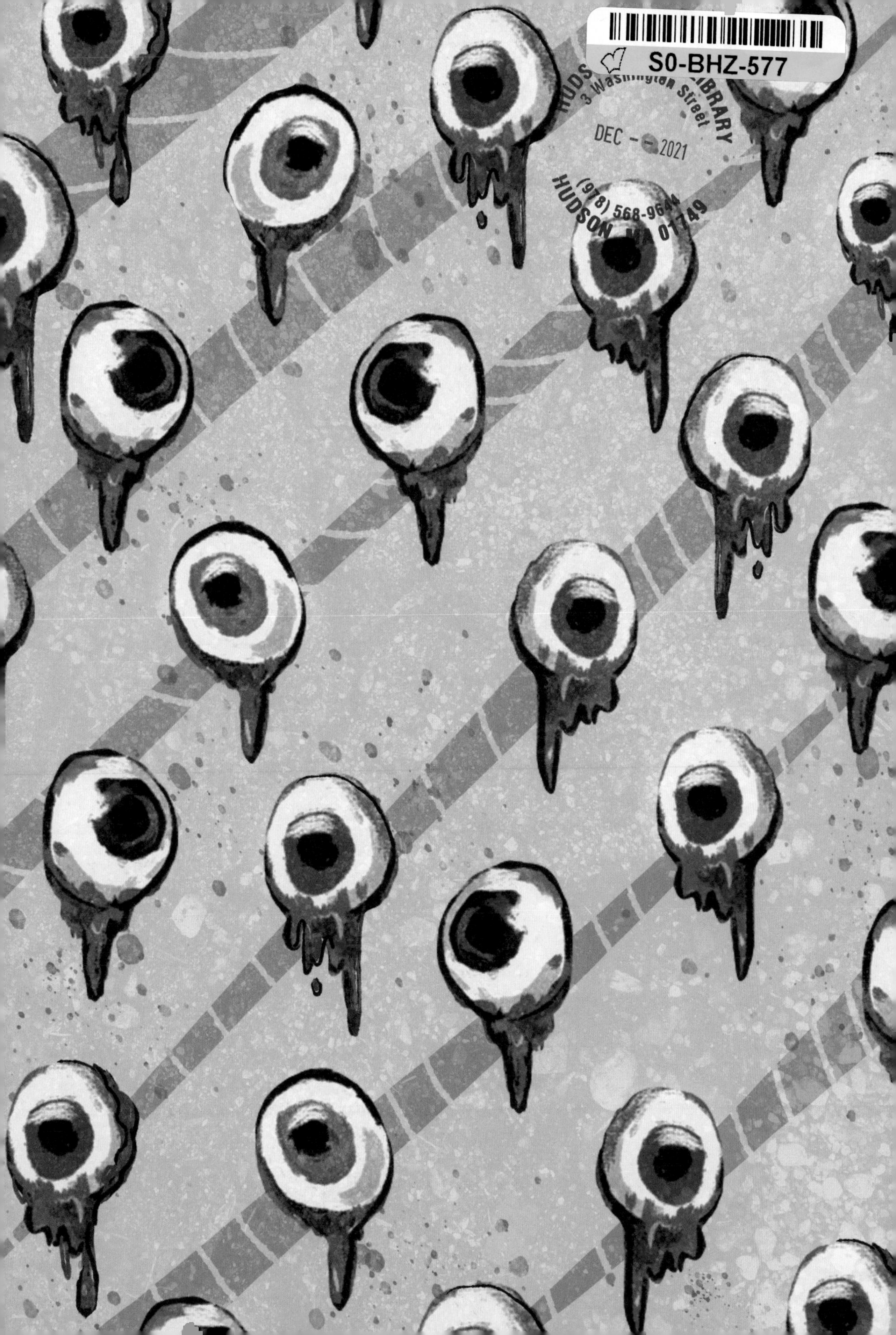

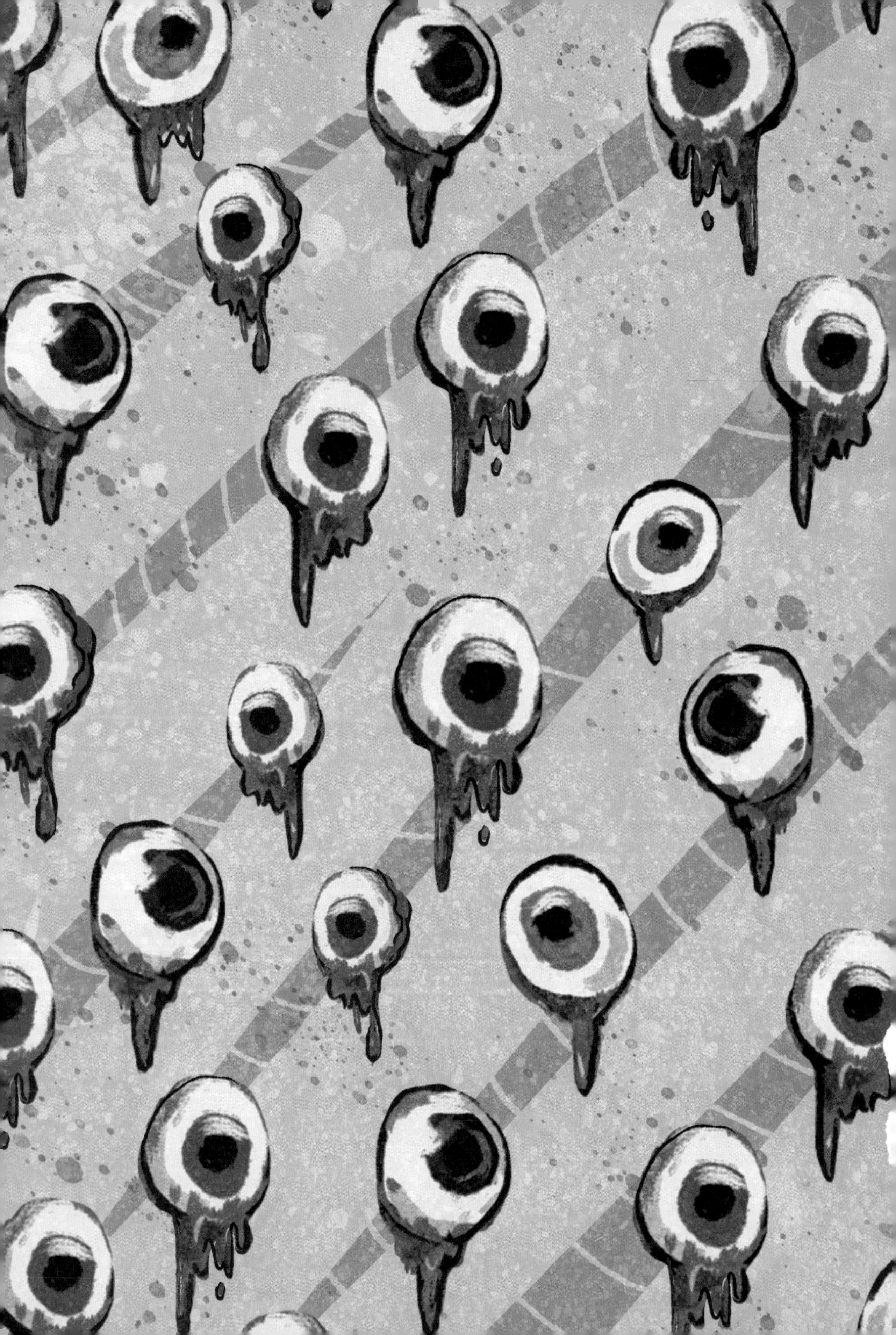

IF UR STABBY

Kaz Windness

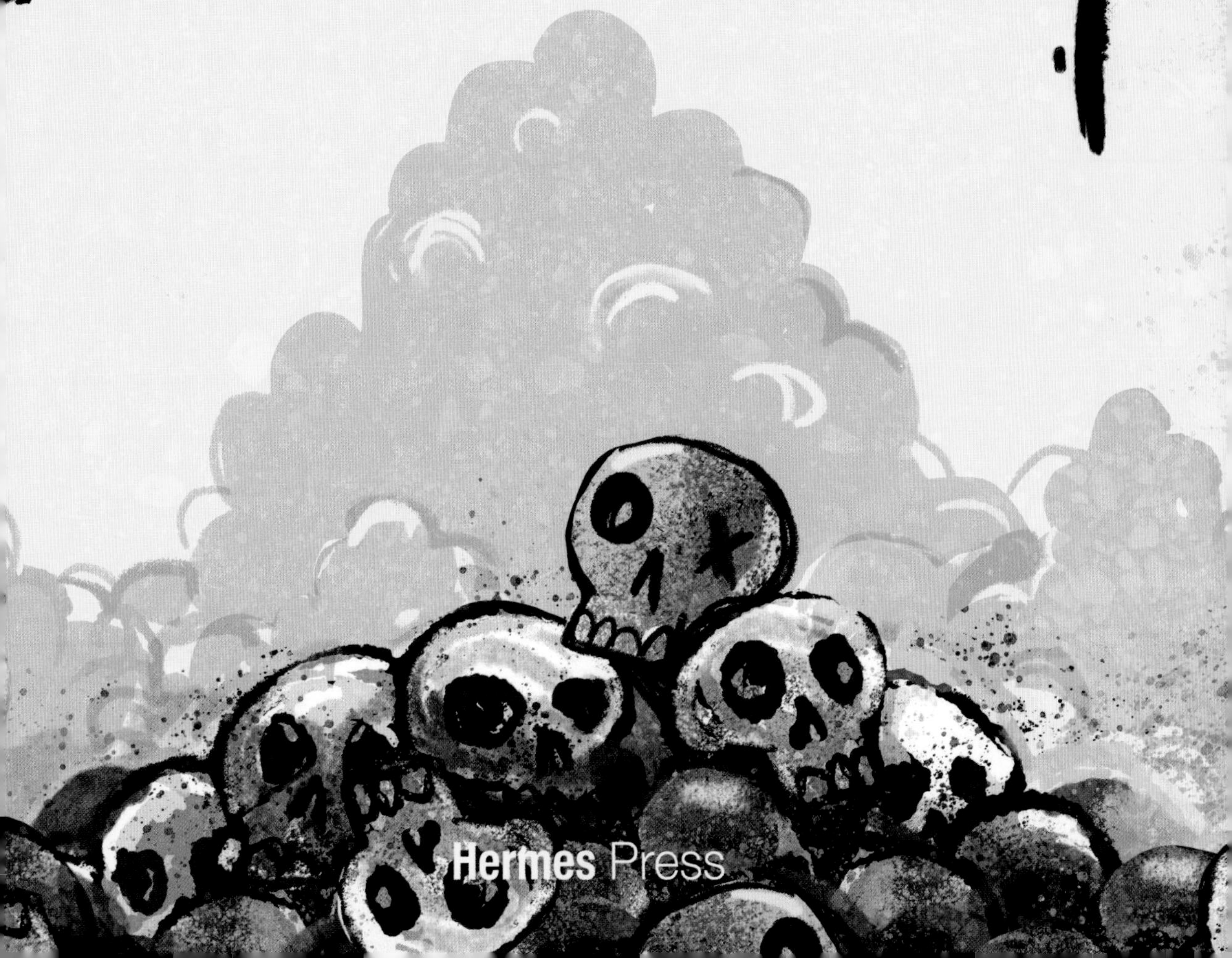

Hermes Press

Once upon a time, there was a murderous unicorn...

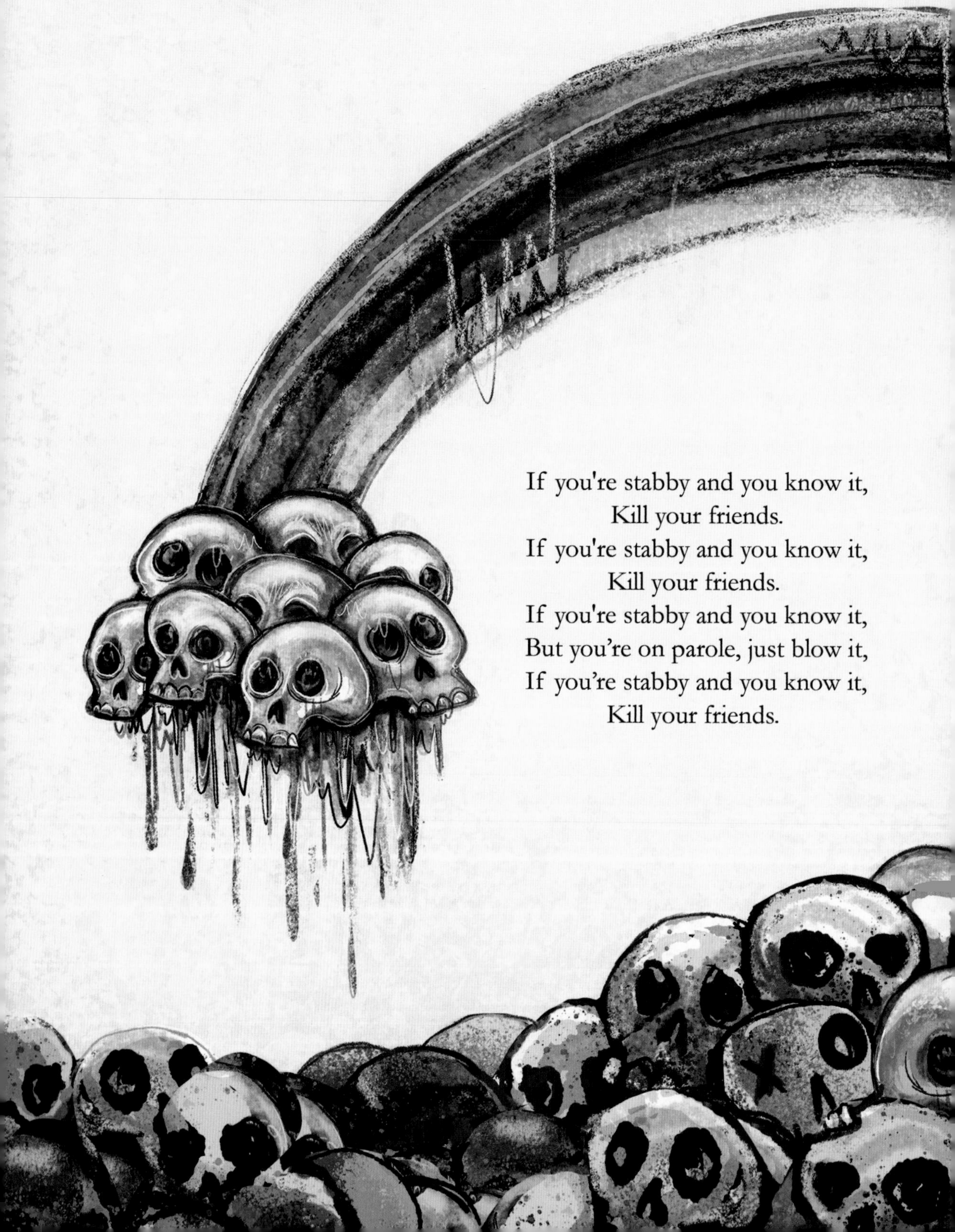

If you're stabby and you know it,
Kill your friends.
If you're stabby and you know it,
Kill your friends.
If you're stabby and you know it,
But you're on parole, just blow it,
If you're stabby and you know it,
Kill your friends.

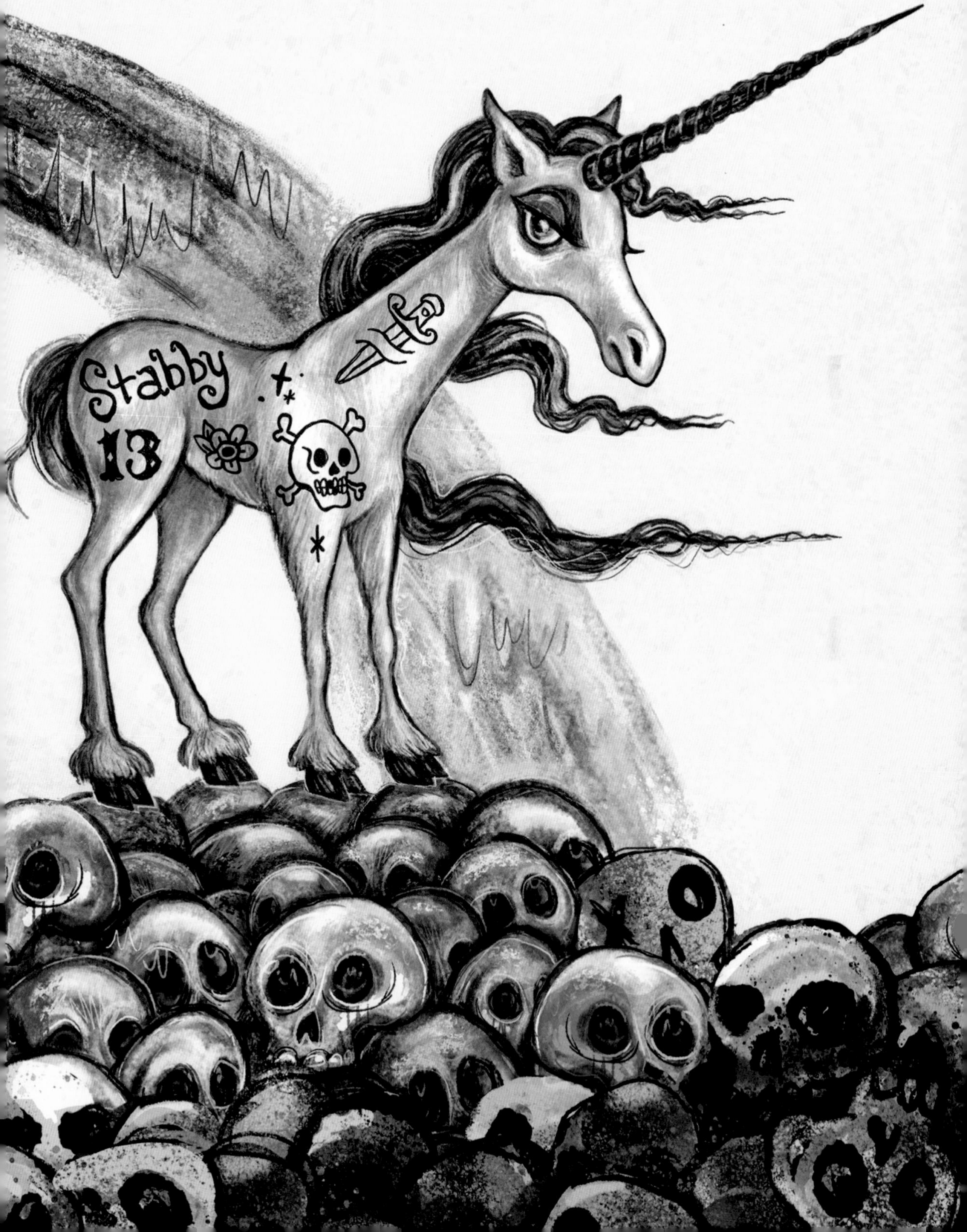
Stabby
13

Other Unicorns

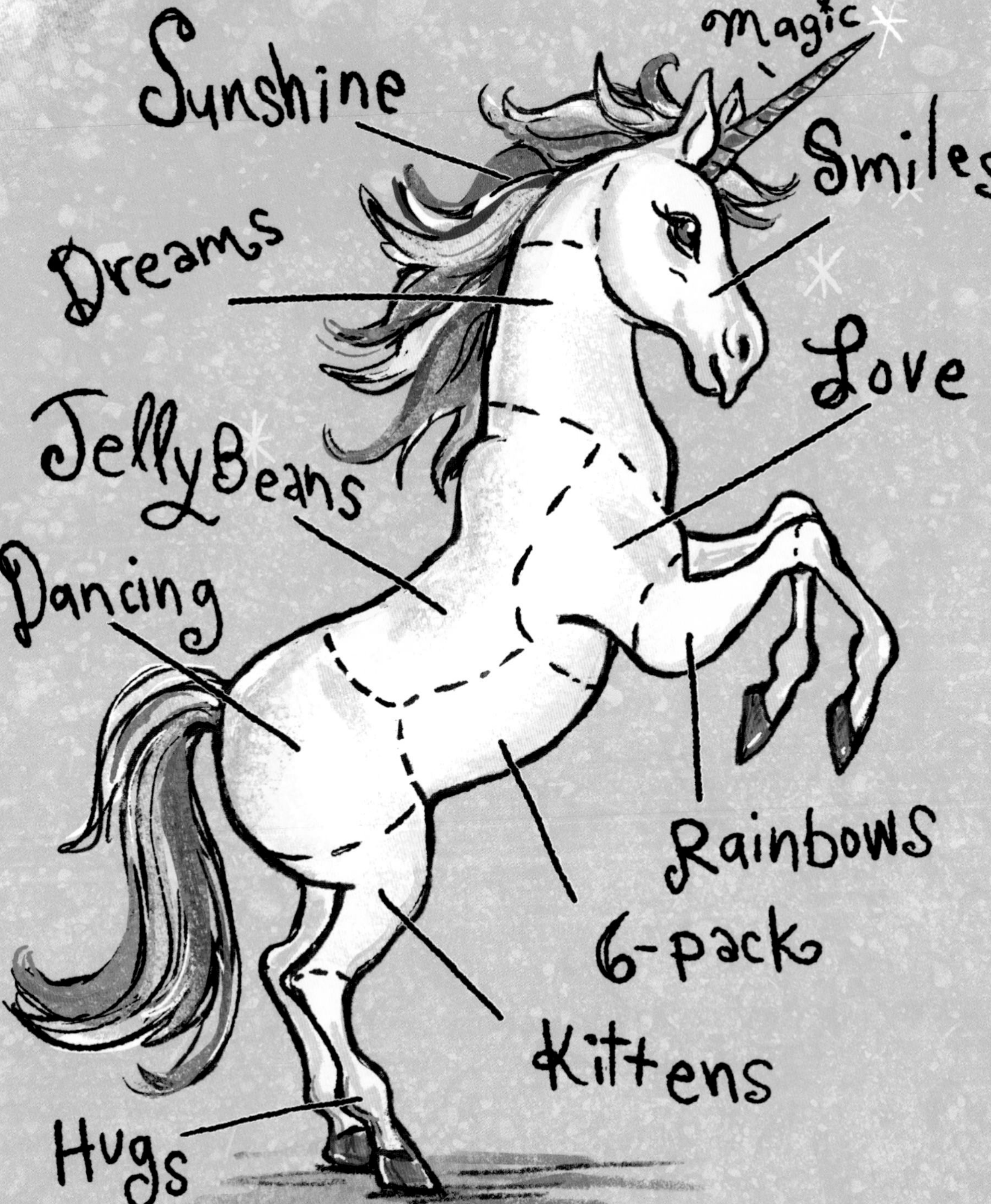
Magic
Sunshine
Smiles
Dreams
Love
JellyBeans
Dancing
Rainbows
6-pack
Kittens
Hugs

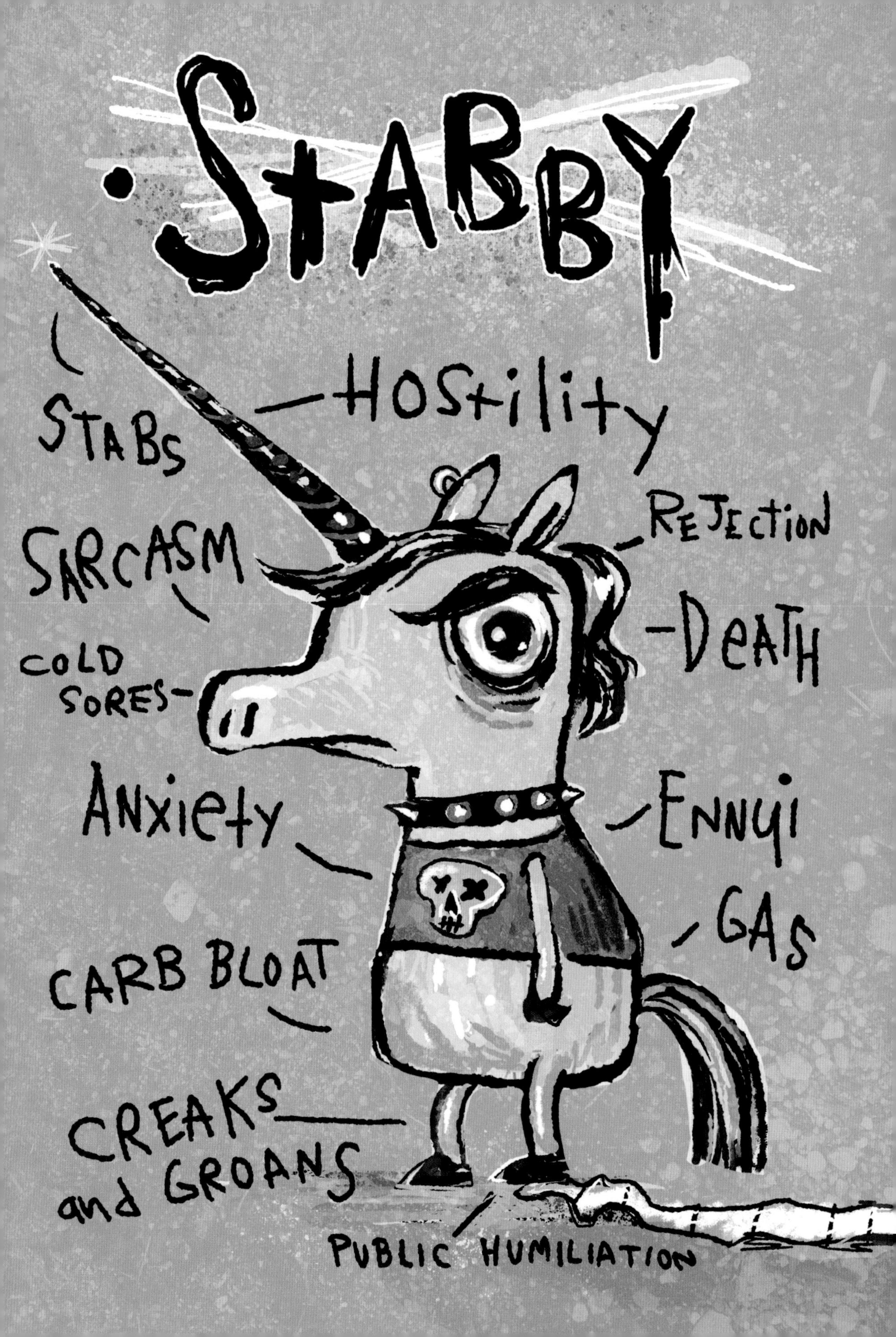
STABBY
STABS
HOStility
REJECTION
SARCASM
-DEATH
COLD SORES-
Anxiety
-Ennui
GAS
CARB BLOAT
CREAKS and GROANS
PUBLIC HUMILIATION

The STABGINNINGS

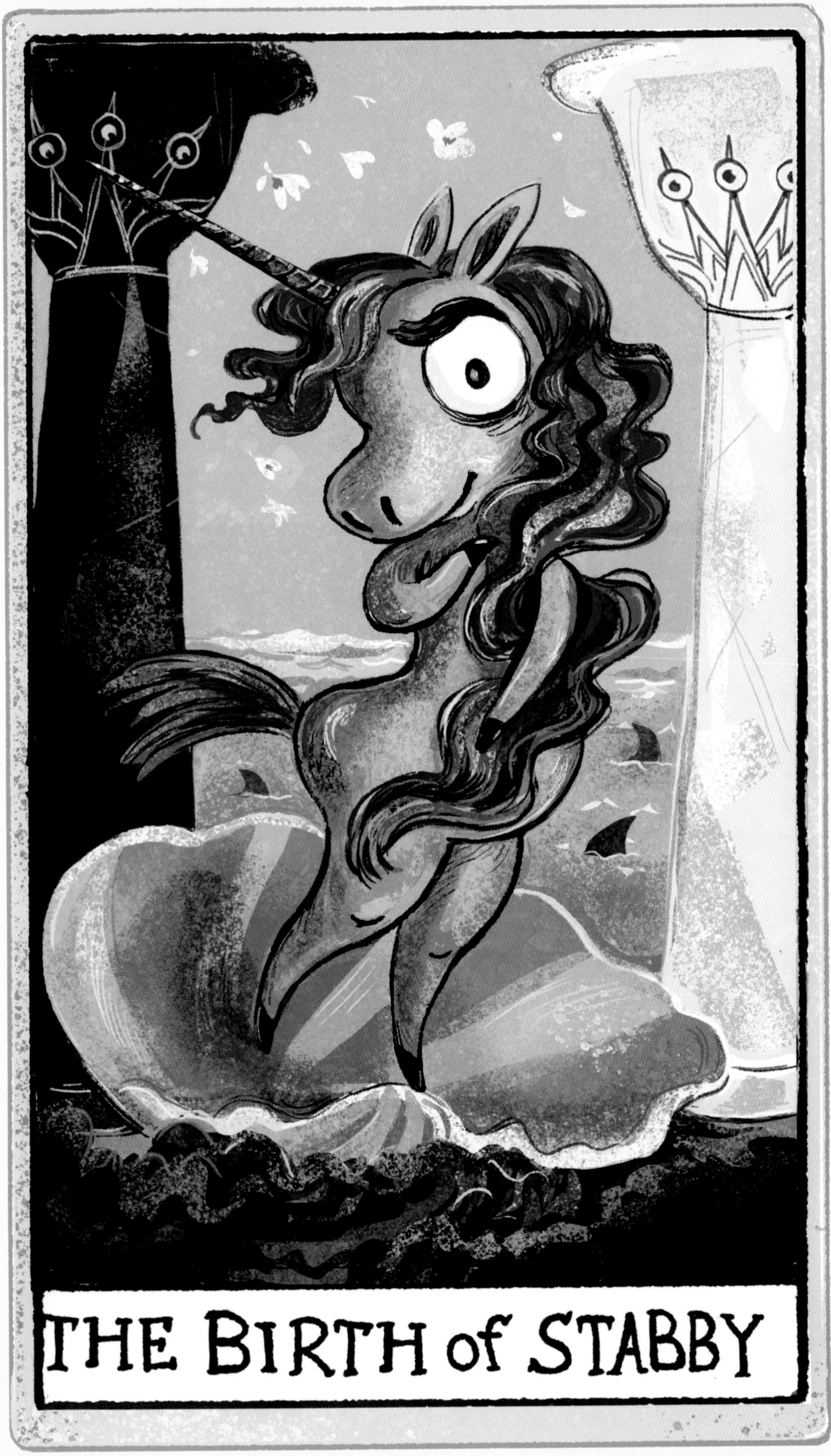
THE BIRTH of STABBY

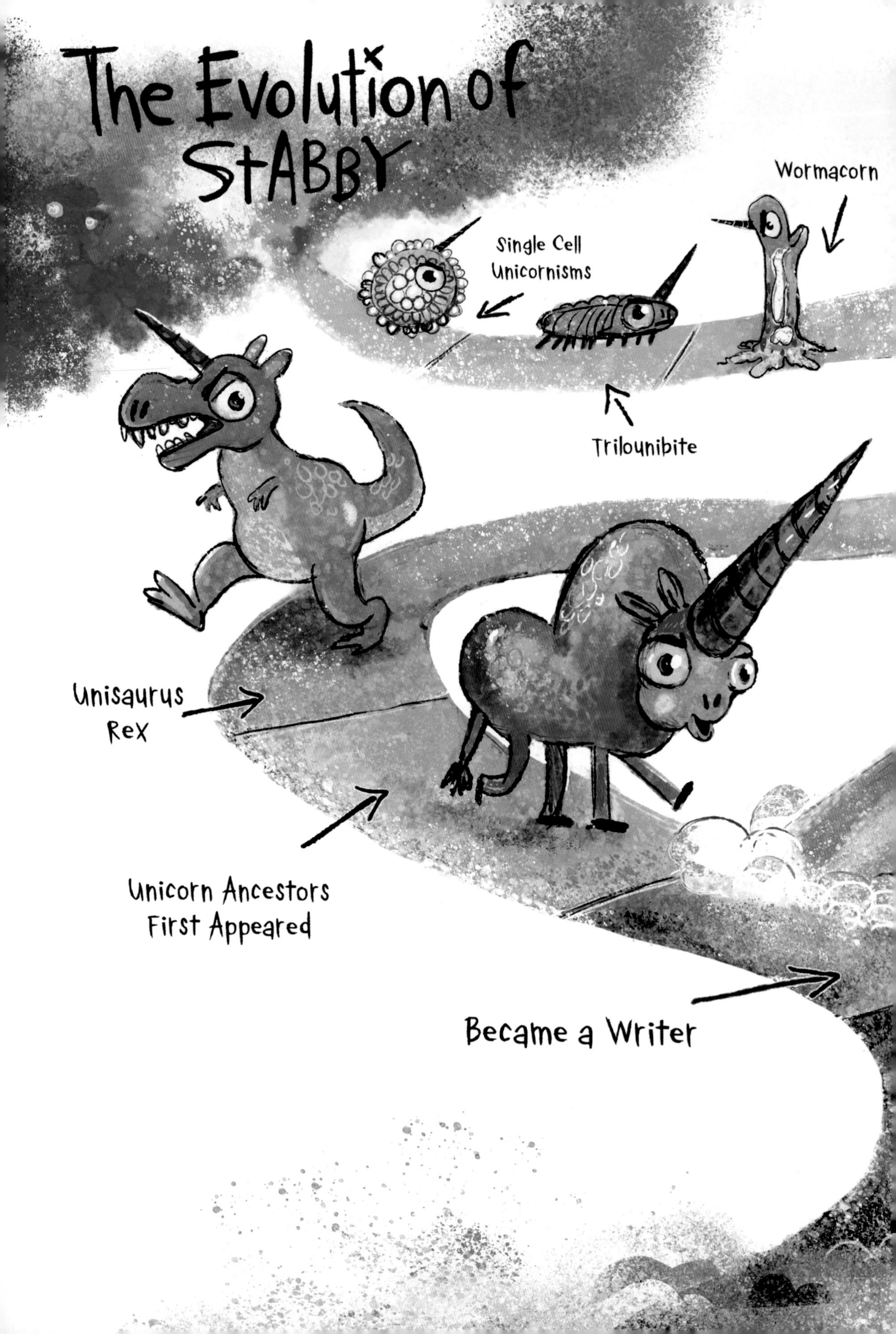
The Evolution of StABBY
Wormacorn
Single Cell Unicornisms
Trilounibite
Unisaurus Rex
Unicorn Ancestors First Appeared
Became a Writer

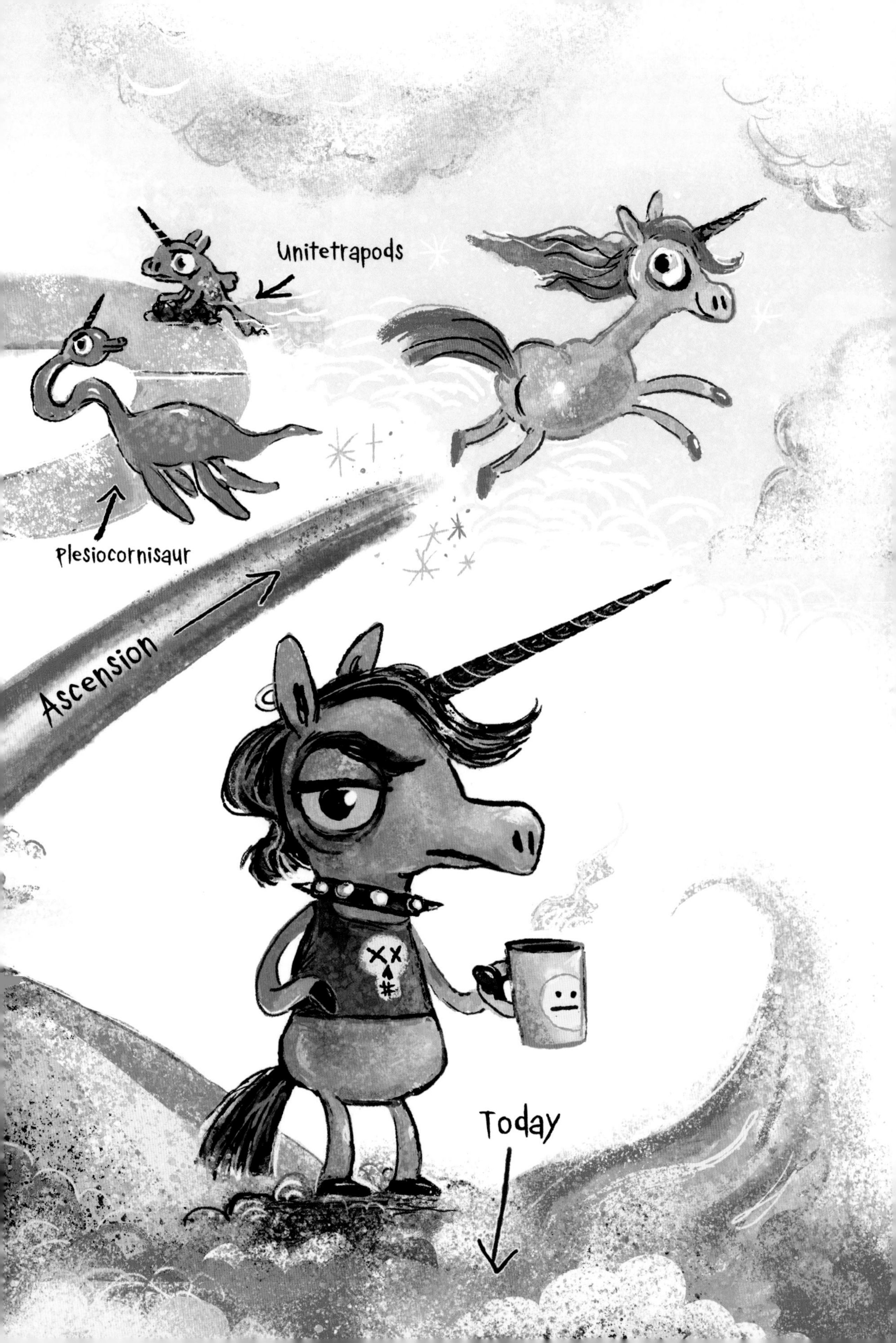
Unitetrapods
Plesiocornisaur
Ascension
Today

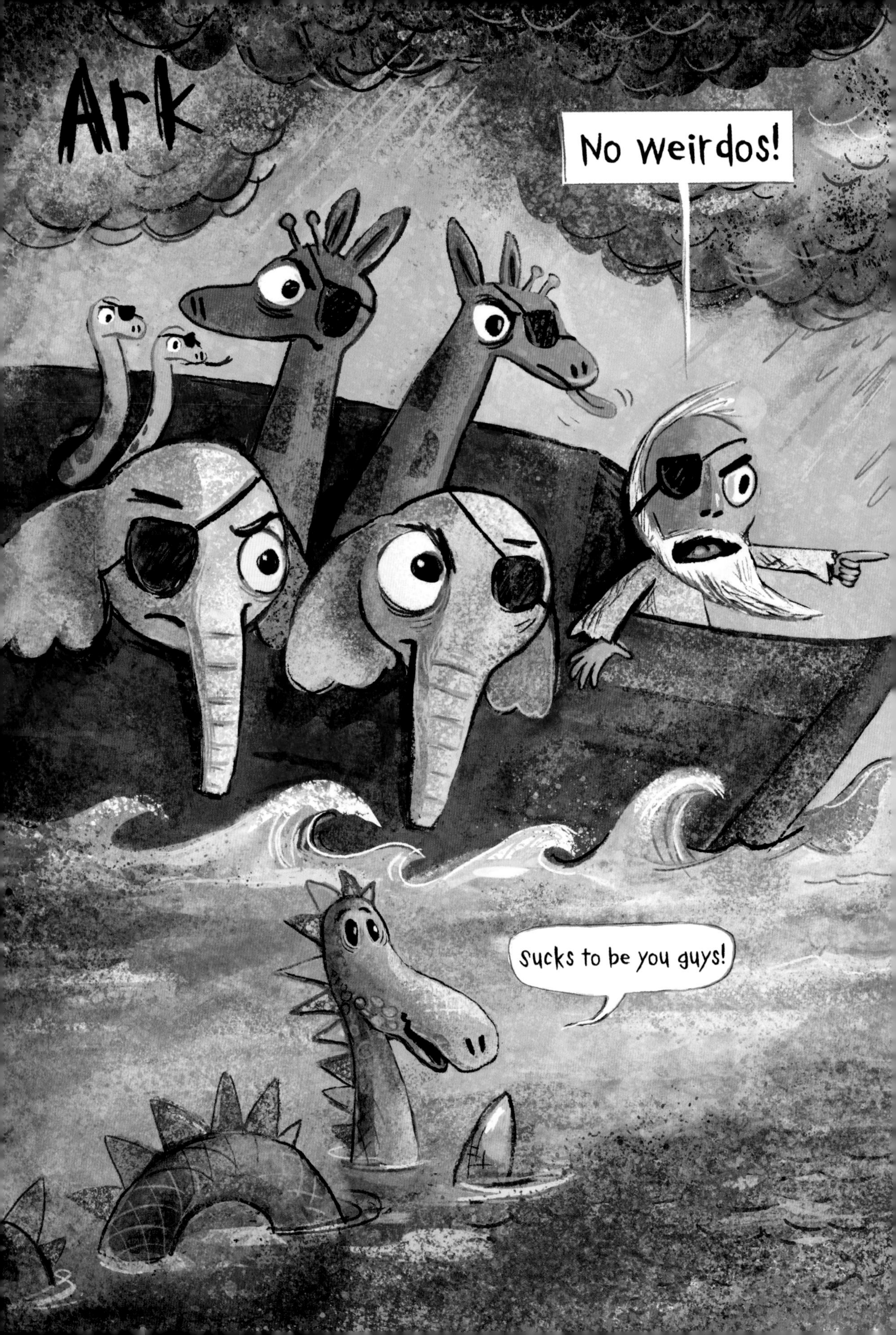
Ark
No weirdos!
sucks to be you guys!

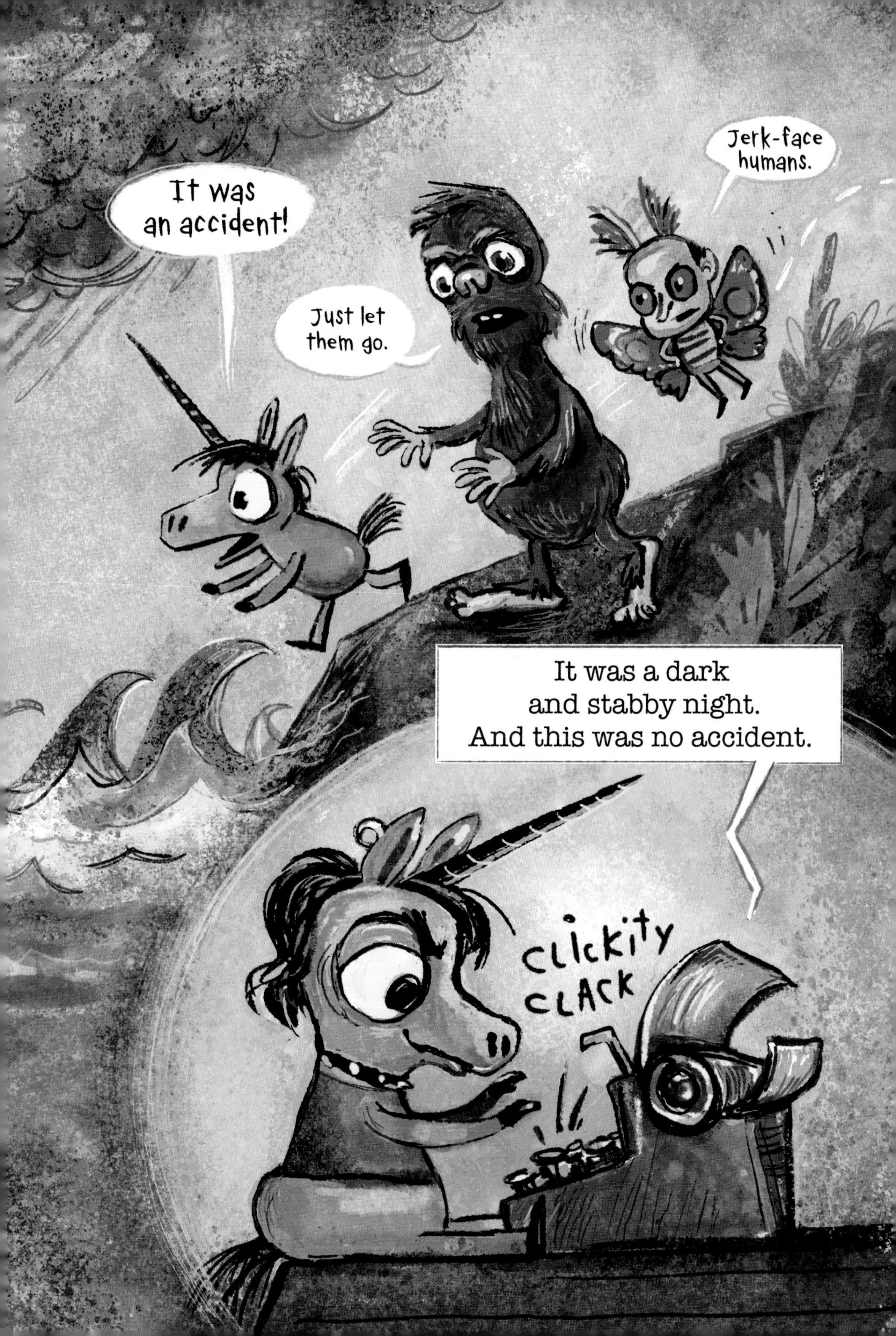

It was an accident!
Just let them go.
Jerk-face humans.
It was a dark and stabby night. And this was no accident.
clickity clack

Career Fails

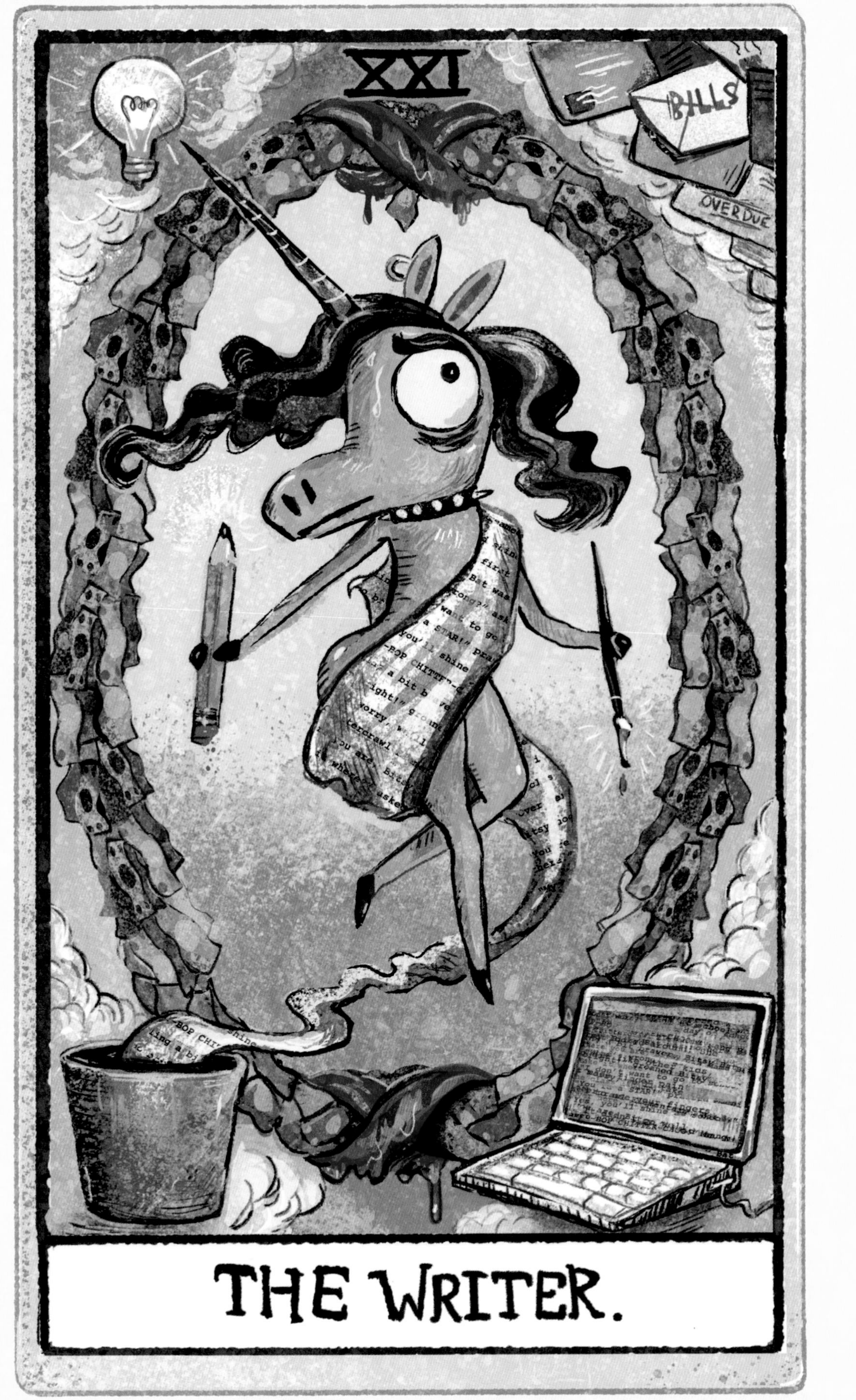
XXI
BILLS
OVERDUE
THE WRITER.

JOB FAILS

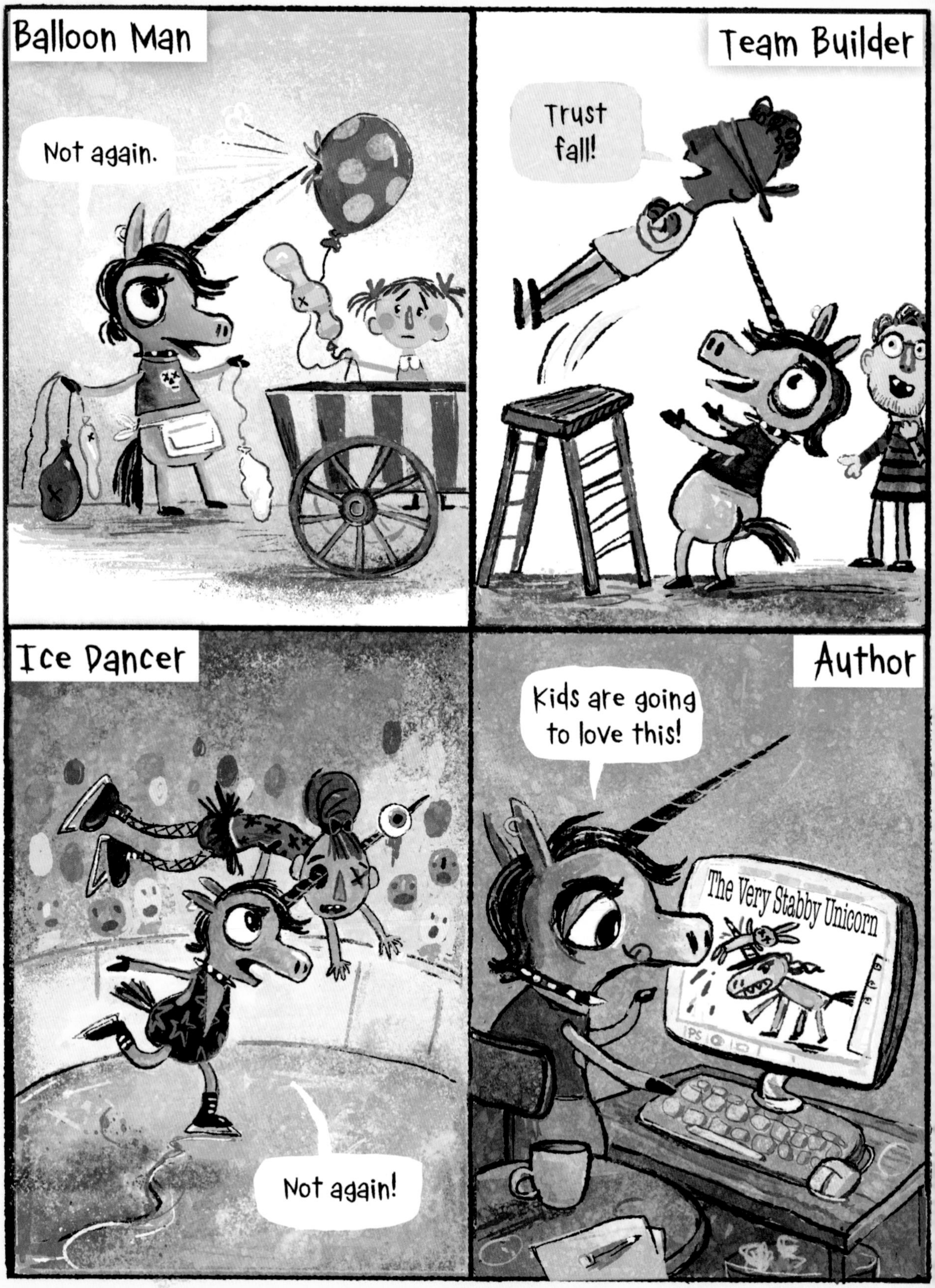
Balloon Man
Not again.
Team Builder
Trust fall!
Ice Dancer
Not again!
Author
Kids are going to love this!
The Very Stabby Unicorn

The Dentist

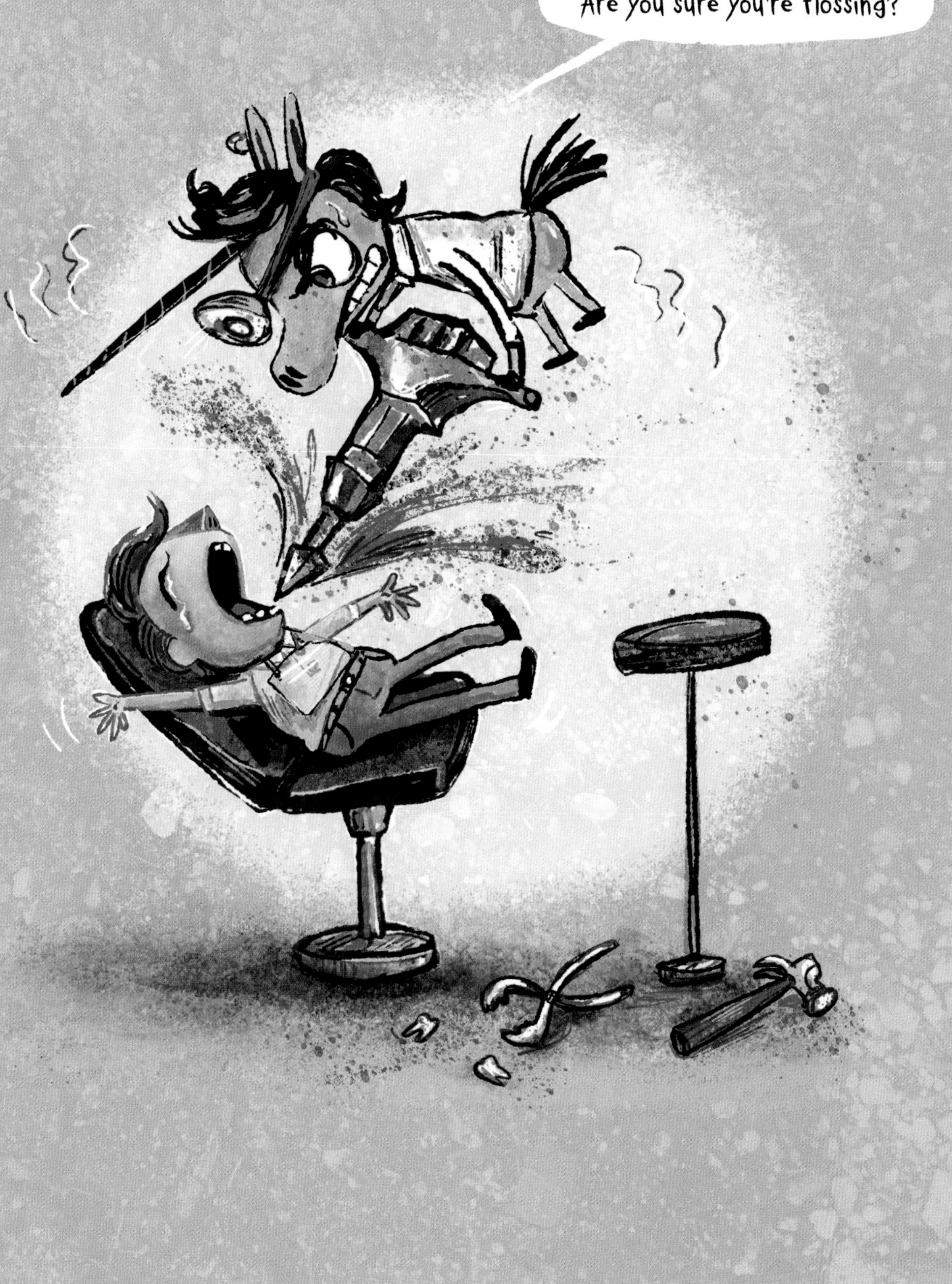
Your gums are bleeding.
Are you sure you're flossing?

Mad Scientist

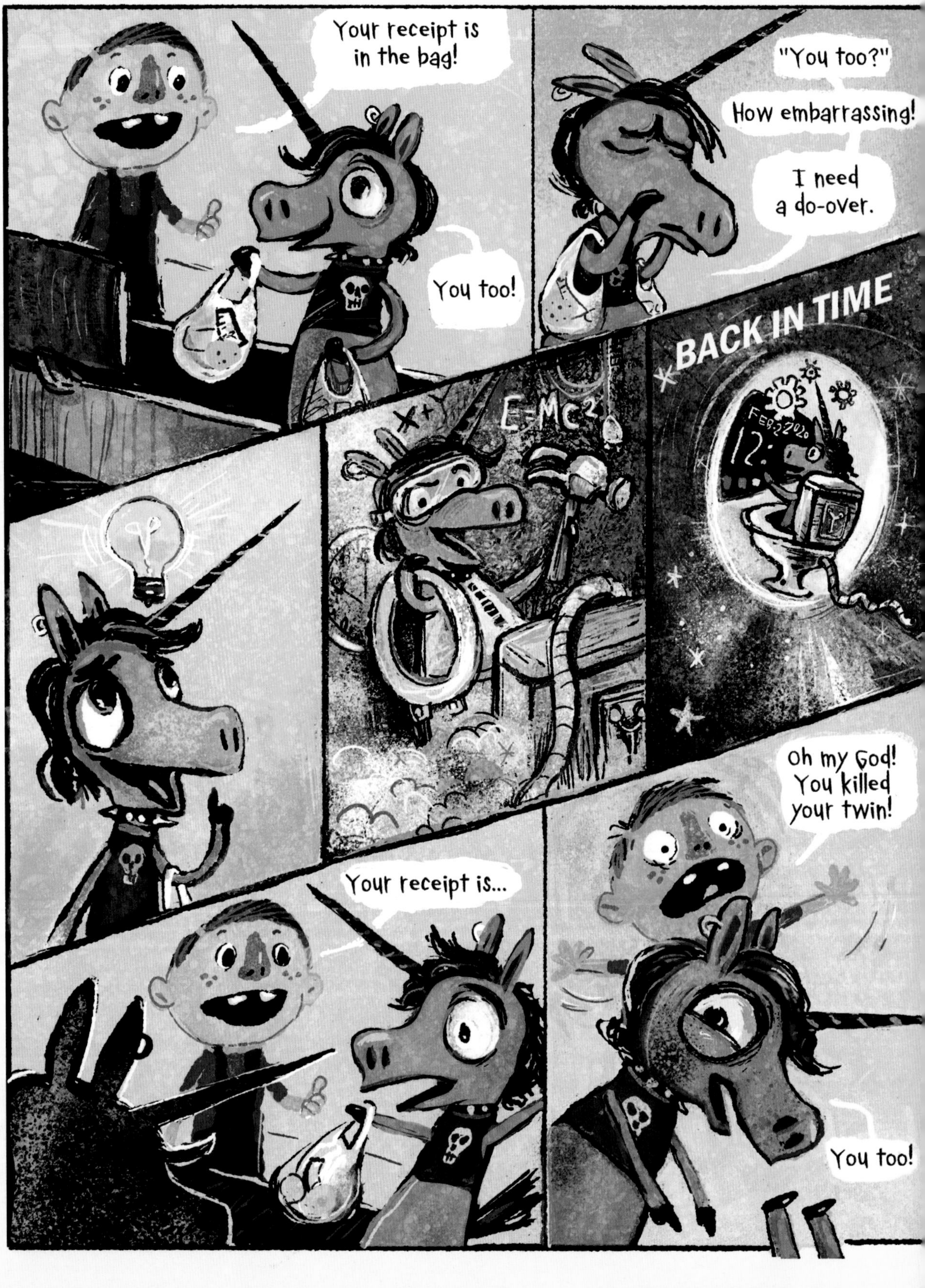
Your receipt is in the bag!
You too!
"You too?"
How embarrassing!
I need a do-over.
E=MC²
BACK IN TIME
FEB 2 2020
12:
Your receipt is...
Oh my God! You killed your twin!
You too!

The Model

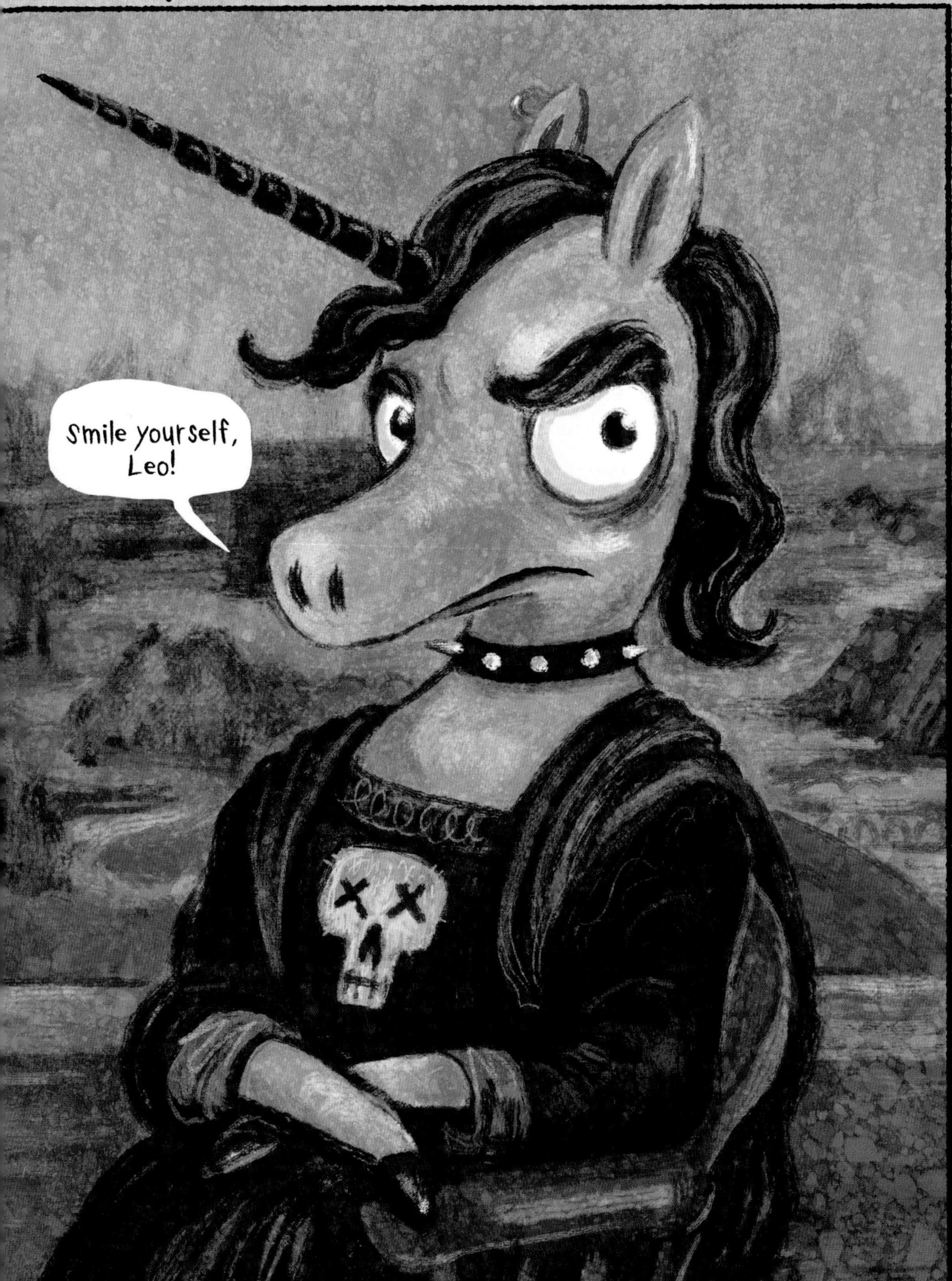
Smile yourself, Leo!

FLIGHT RISK

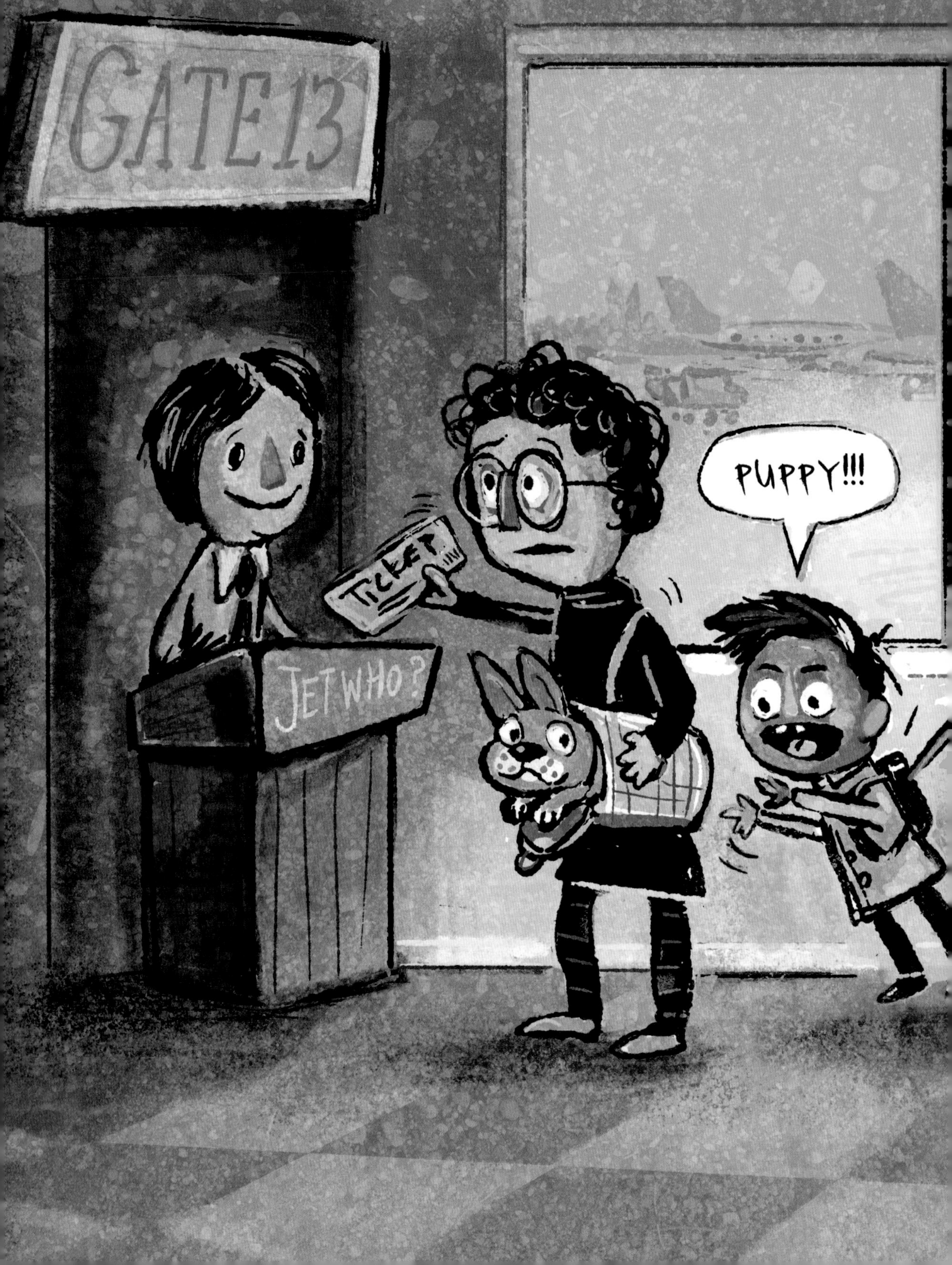
GATE 13
TICKET
JET WHO?
PUPPY!!!

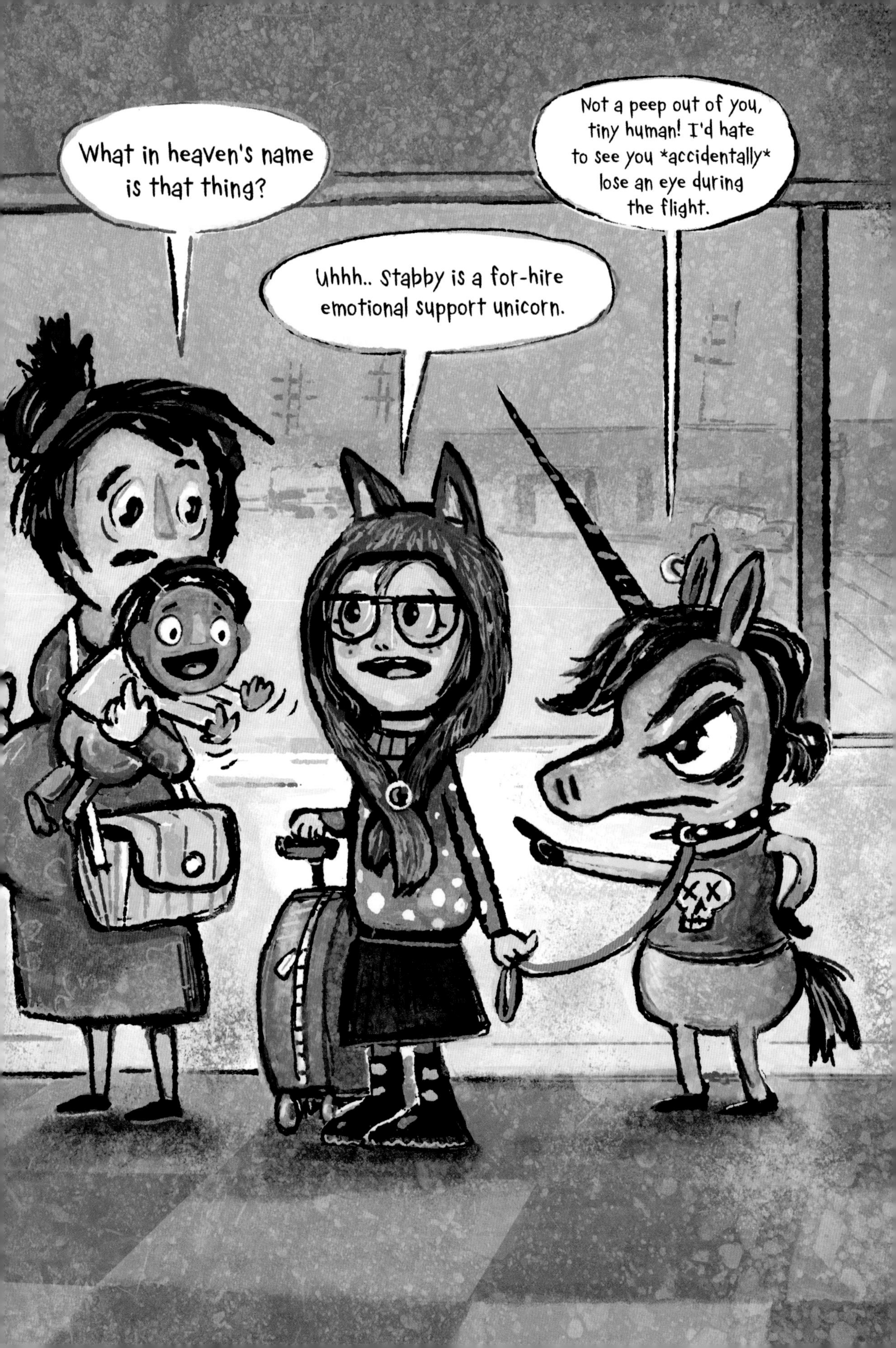
What in heaven's name is that thing?
Uhhh.. Stabby is a for-hire emotional support unicorn.
Not a peep out of you, tiny human! I'd hate to see you *accidentally* lose an eye during the flight.

HANGRY

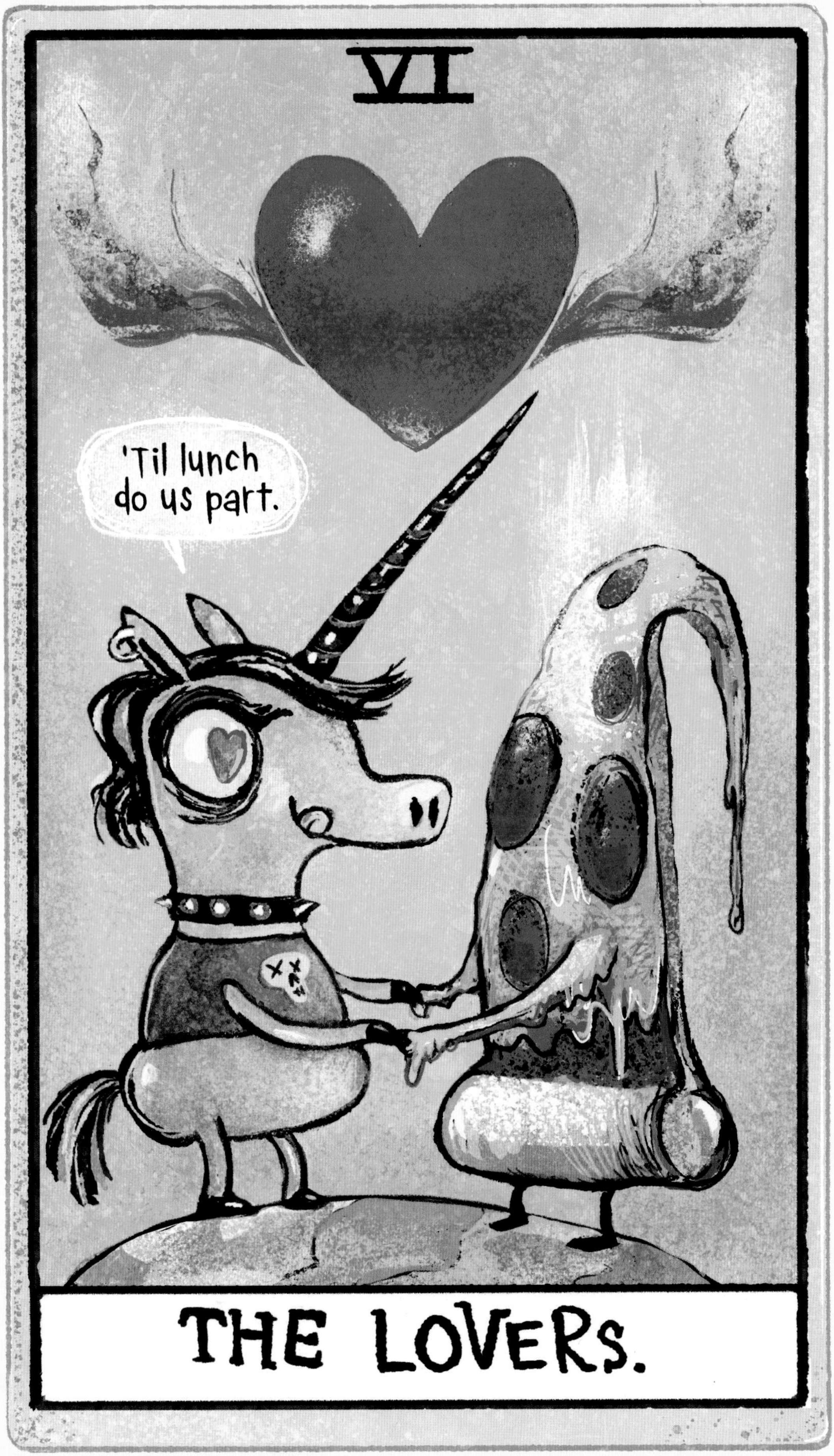
VI
'Til lunch do us part.
THE LOVERS.

The SPiCE

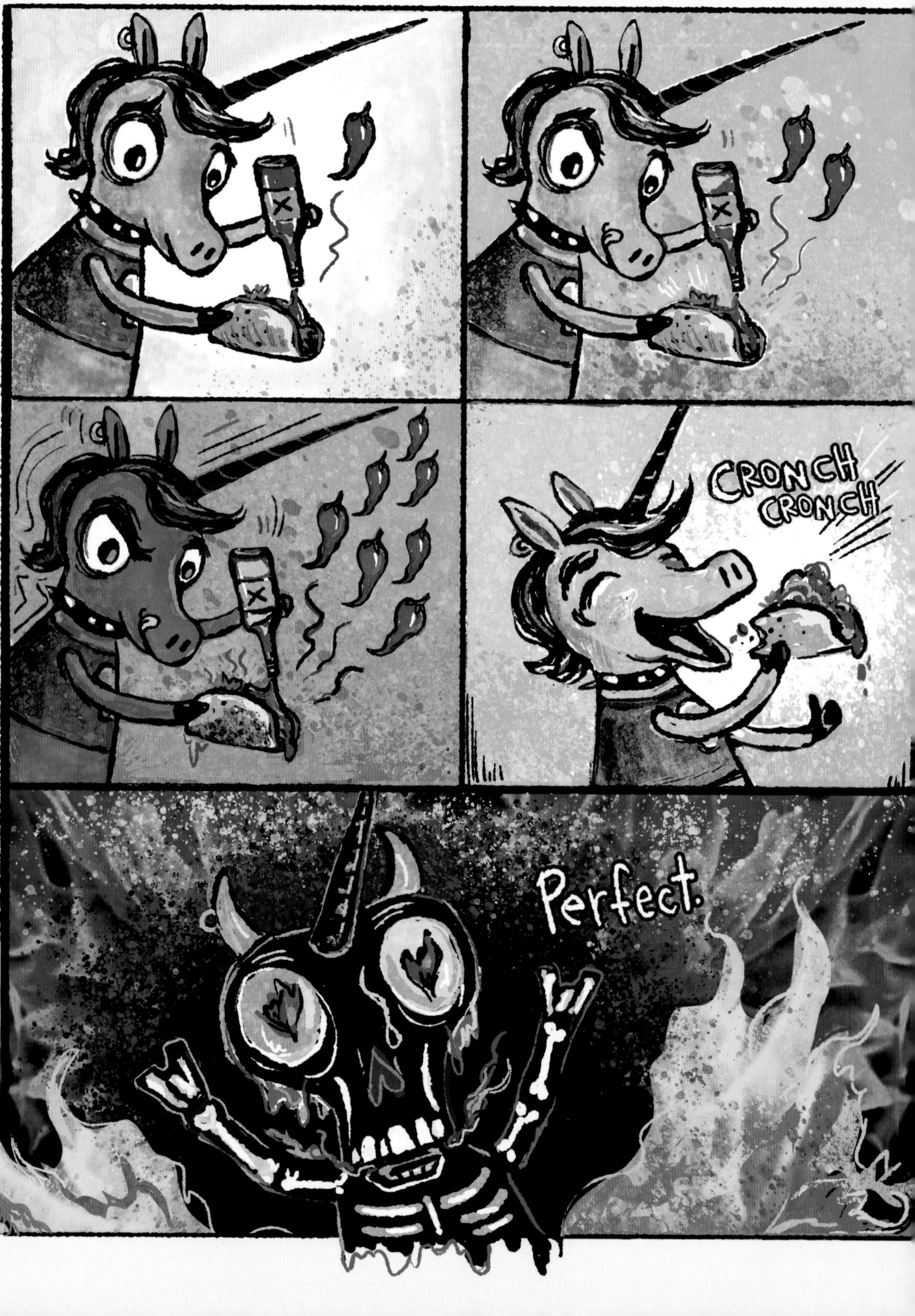
CRONCH
CRONCH
Perfect.

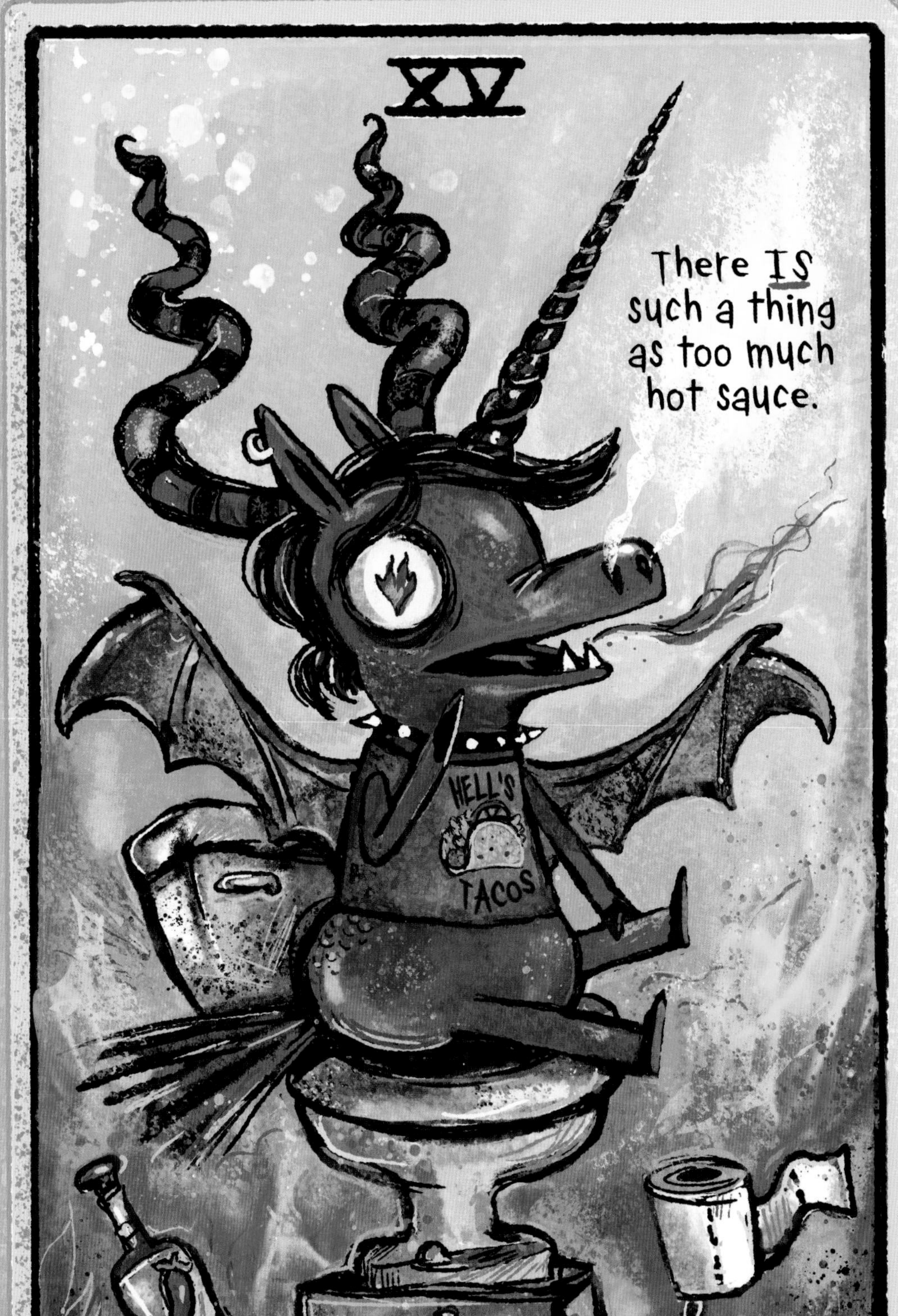
XV
There IS such a thing as too much hot sauce.
HELL'S TACOS
THE DEVIL.

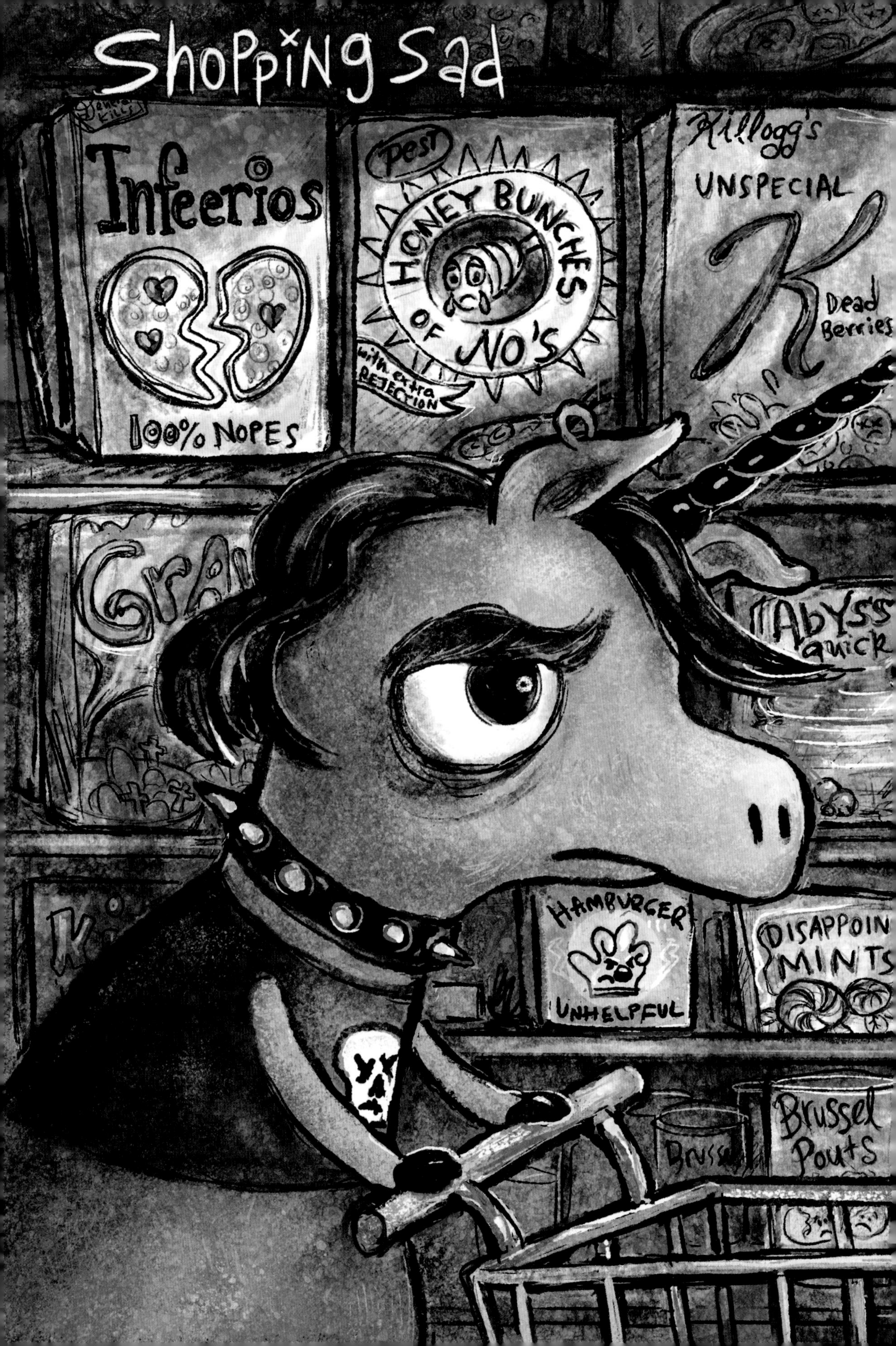
Shopping Sad
Infeerios
100% NOPES
Pest
HONEY BUNCHES OF NO'S
with extra REJECTION
Killogg's
UNSPECIAL
K
Dead Berries
Abyss quick
HAMBURGER
UNHELPFUL
DISAPPOIN MINTS
Brussel Pouts

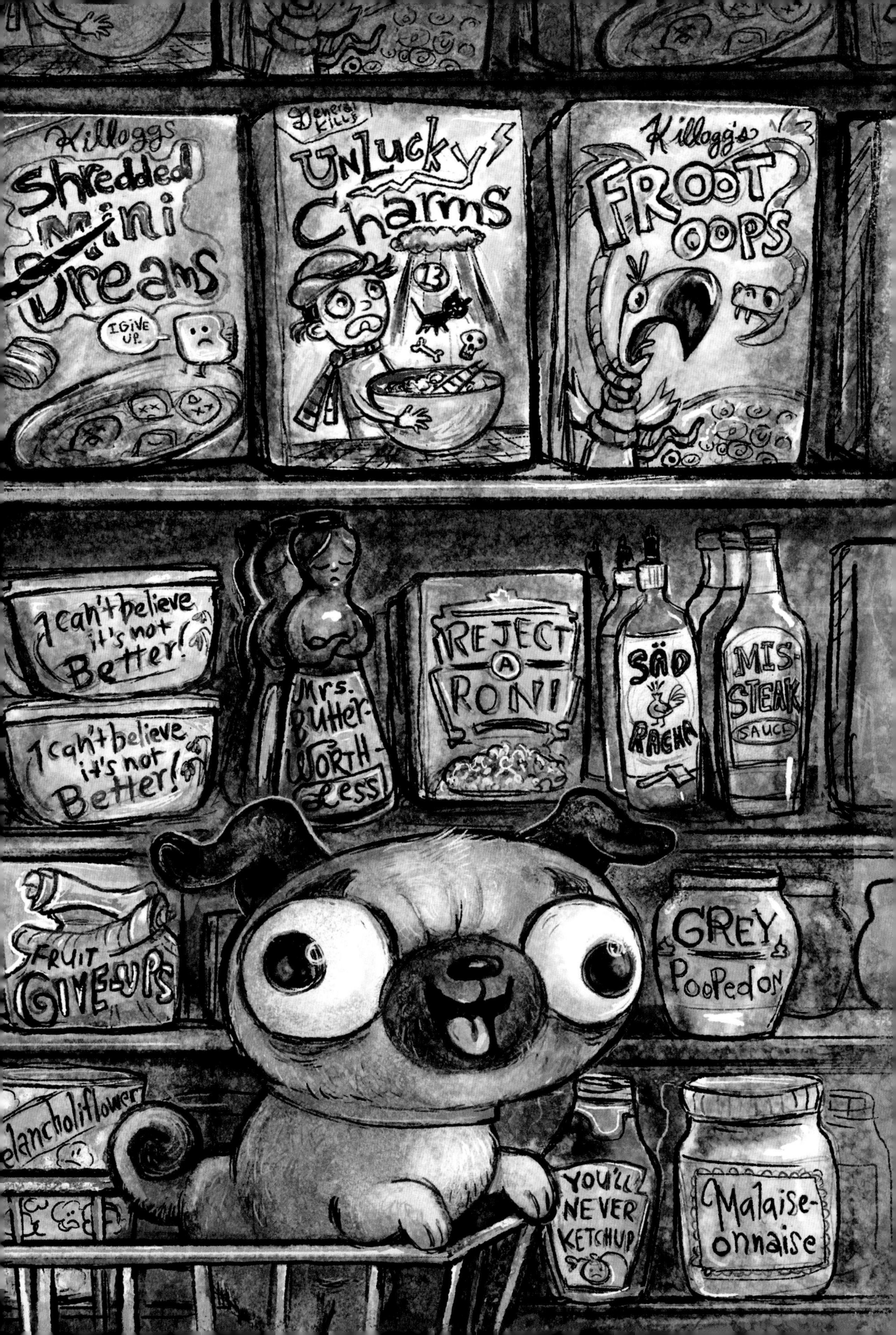
Killoggs
Shredded Mini Dreams
I GIVE UP.
General Kills
UnLucky Charms
13
Killogg's
FROOT OOPS
I can't believe it's not Better!
I can't believe it's not Better!
Mrs. Butter-Worth-Less
REJECT A RONI
SÄD RACHA
MIS-STEAK SAUCE
FRUIT GIVE-UPS
GREY PooPed ON
elancholiflower
YOU'LL NEVER KETCHUP
Malaise-onnaise

MURDEROUS TENDENCIES

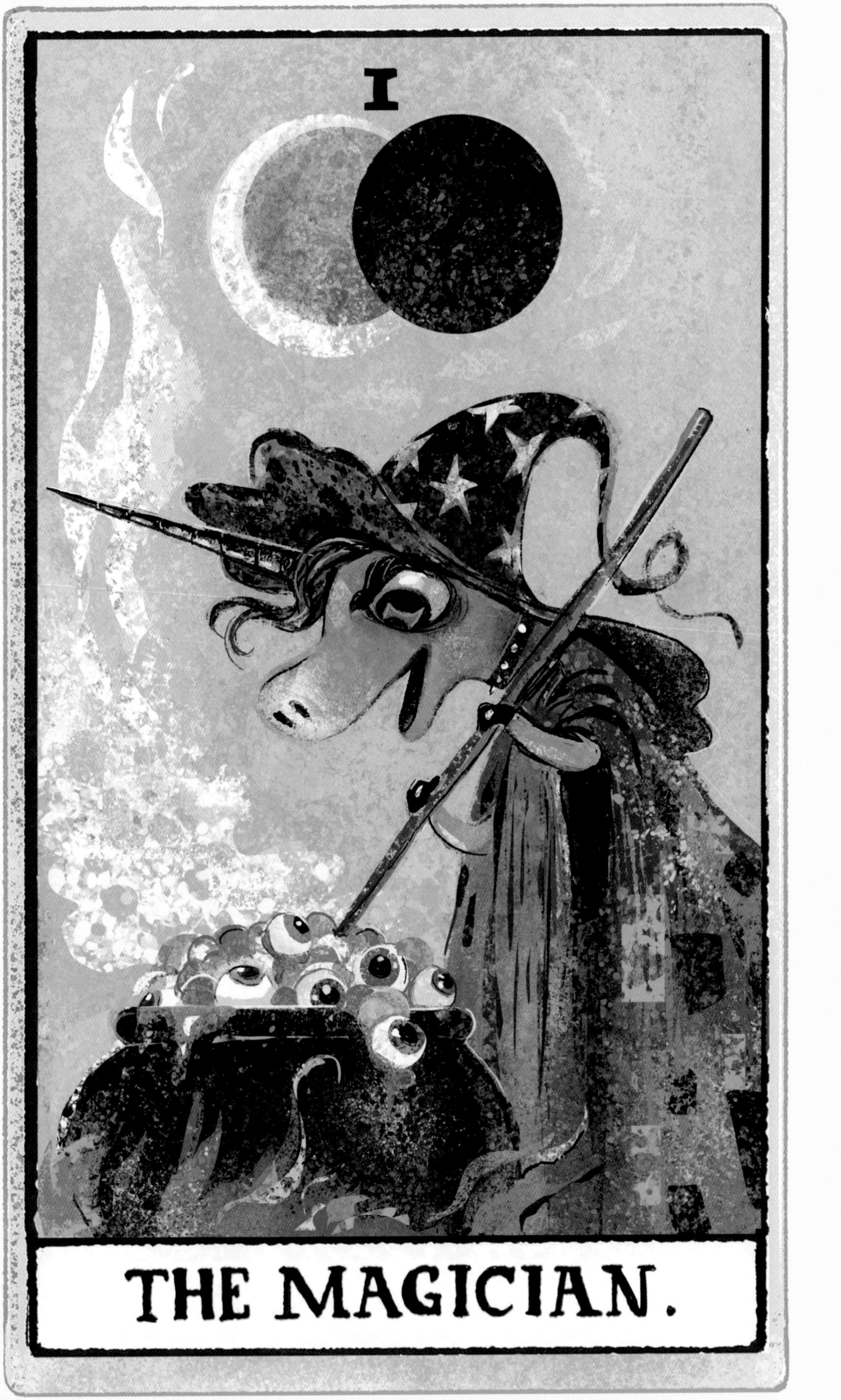
I
THE MAGICIAN.

Lemons

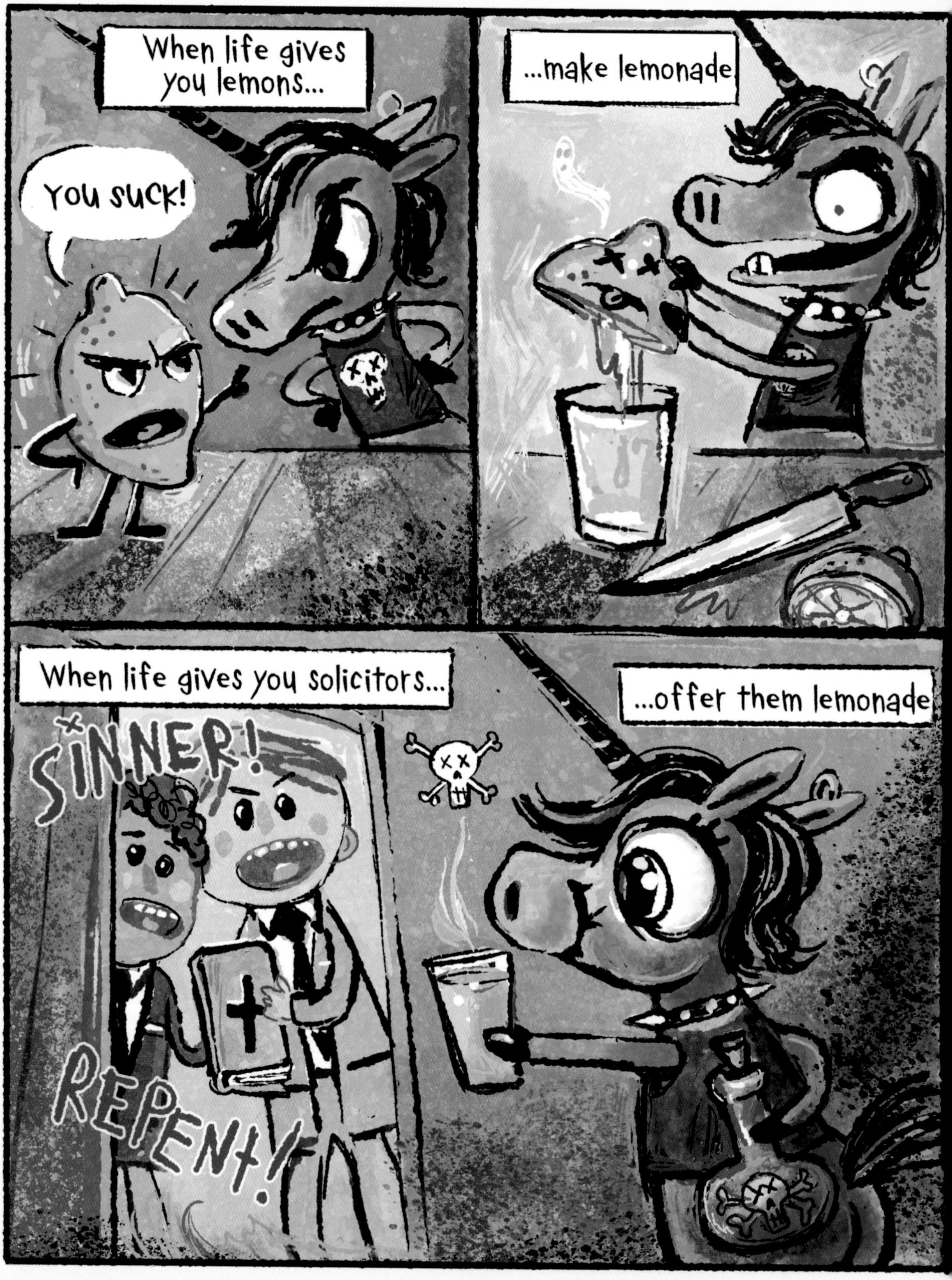
When life gives you lemons...
You suck!
...make lemonade
When life gives you solicitors...
SINNER!
REPENT!
...offer them lemonade

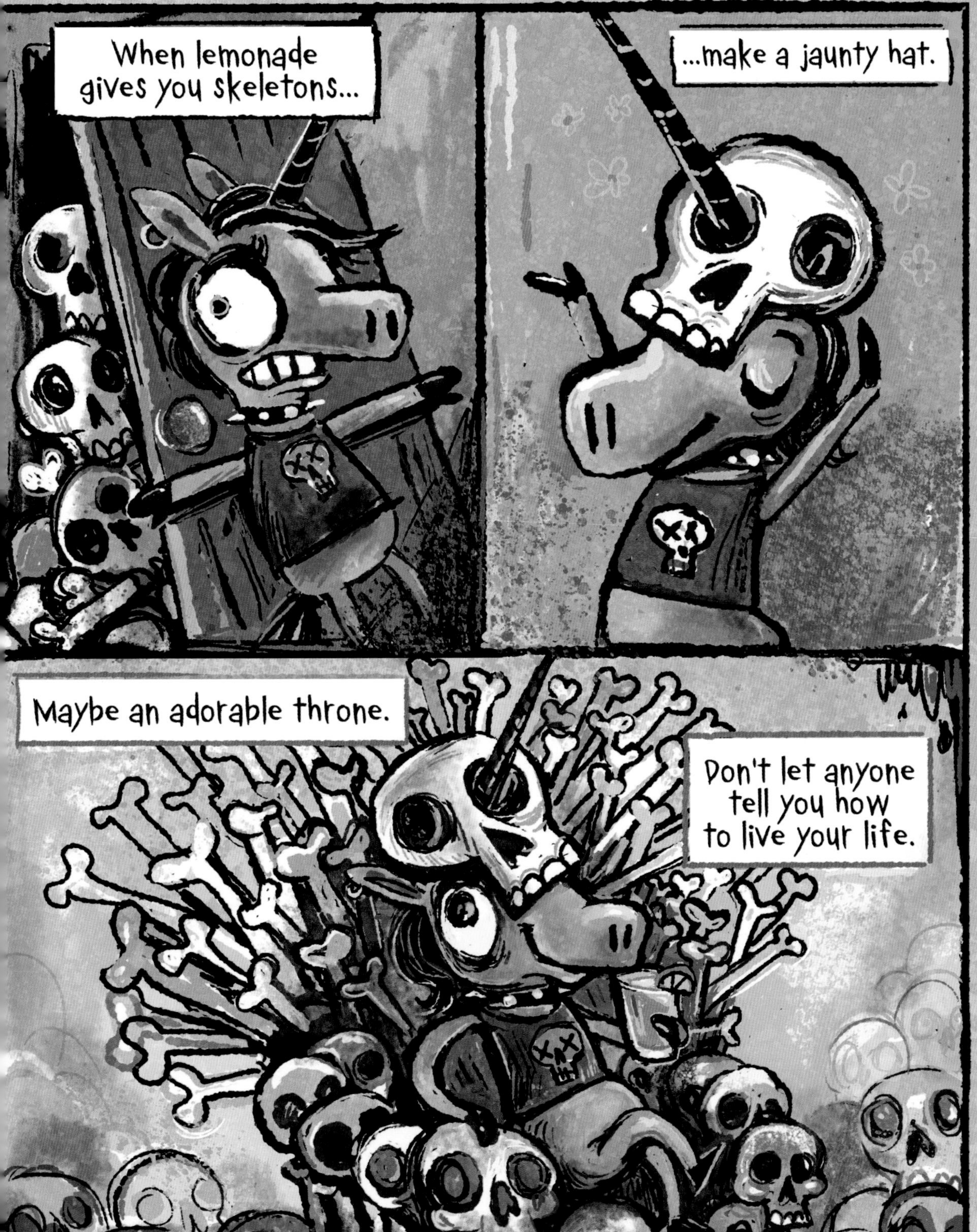
When lemonade gives you skeletons...
...make a jaunty hat.
Maybe an adorable throne.
Don't let anyone tell you how to live your life.

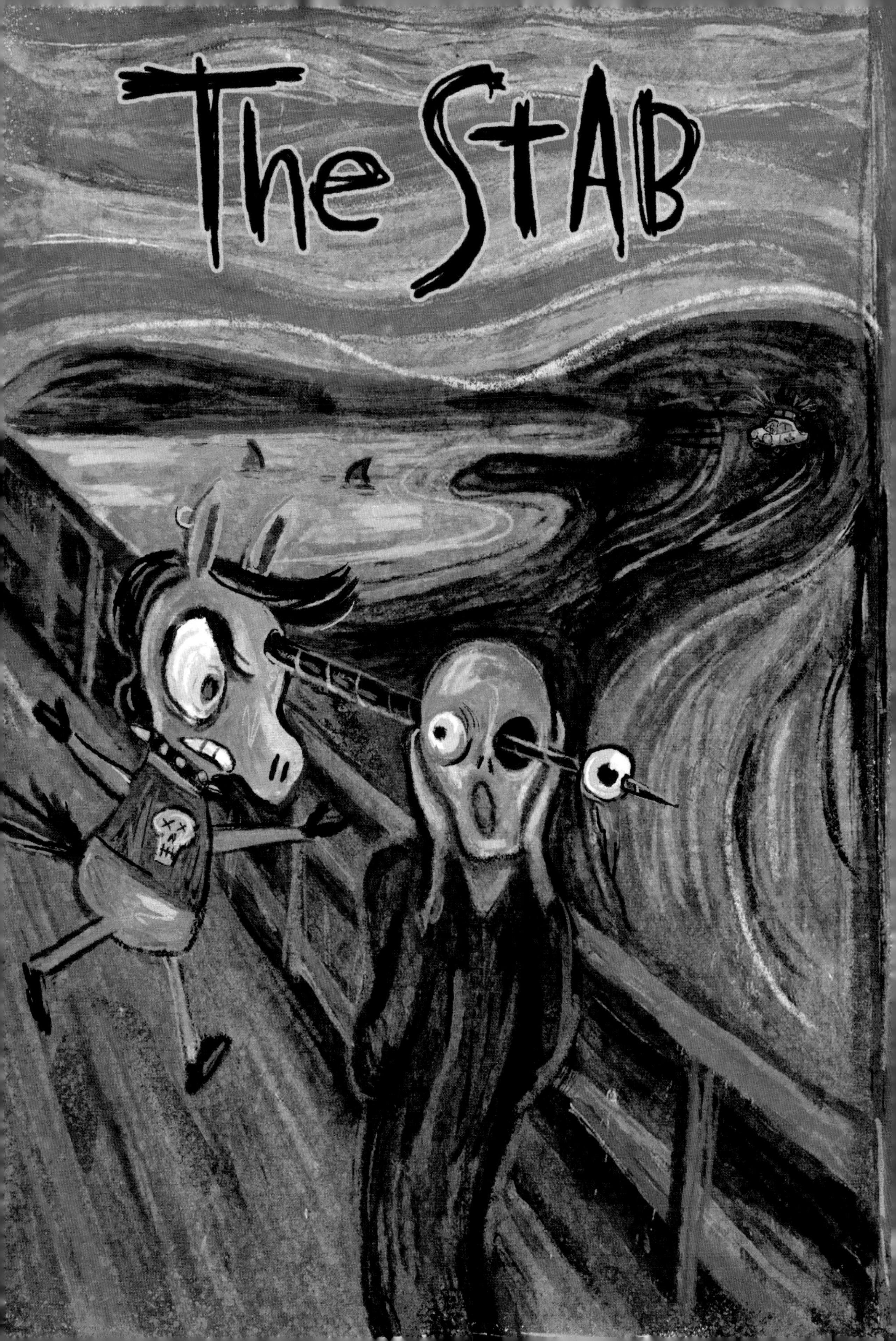
The StAB

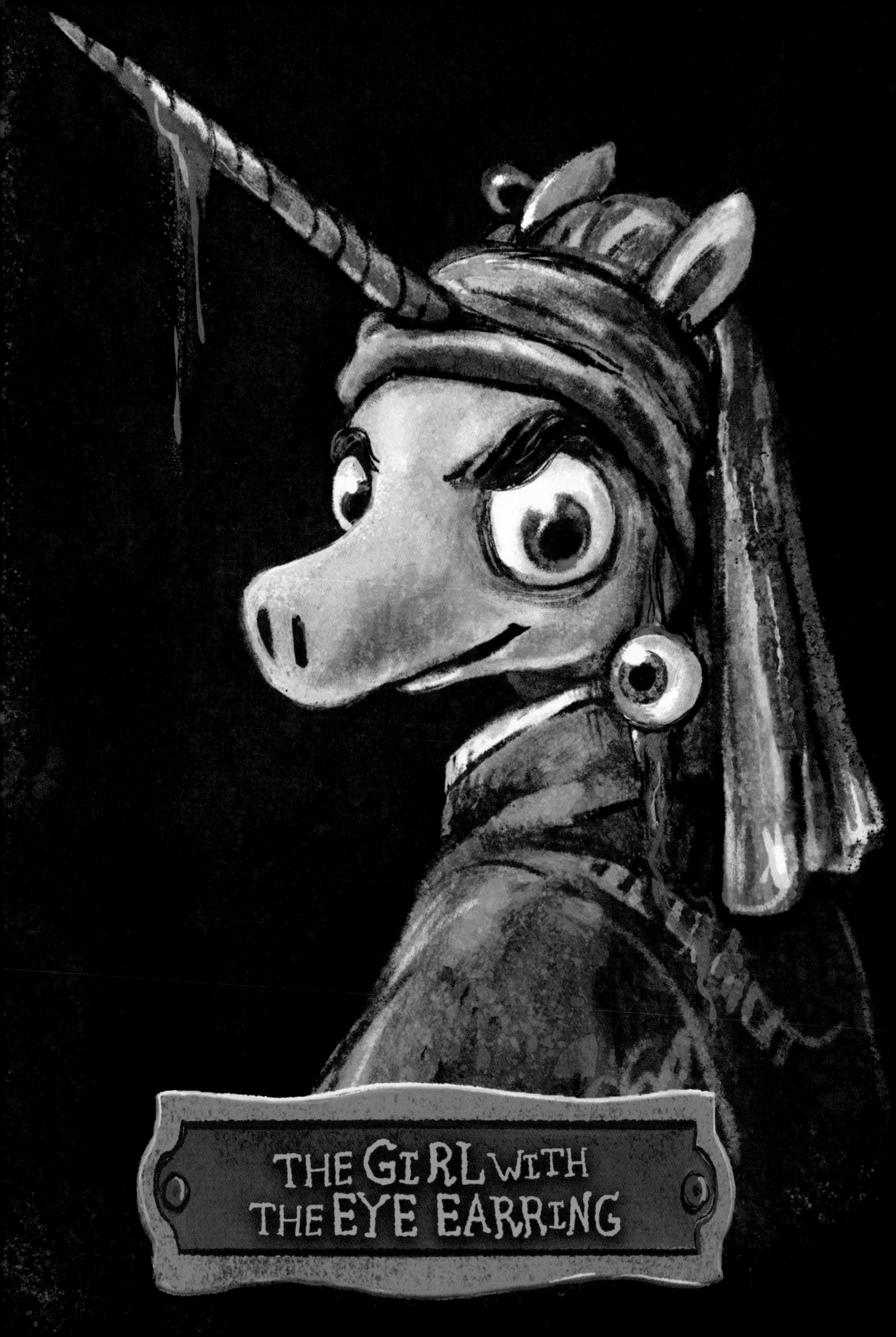
THE GIRL WITH
THE EYE EARRING

PODCAST

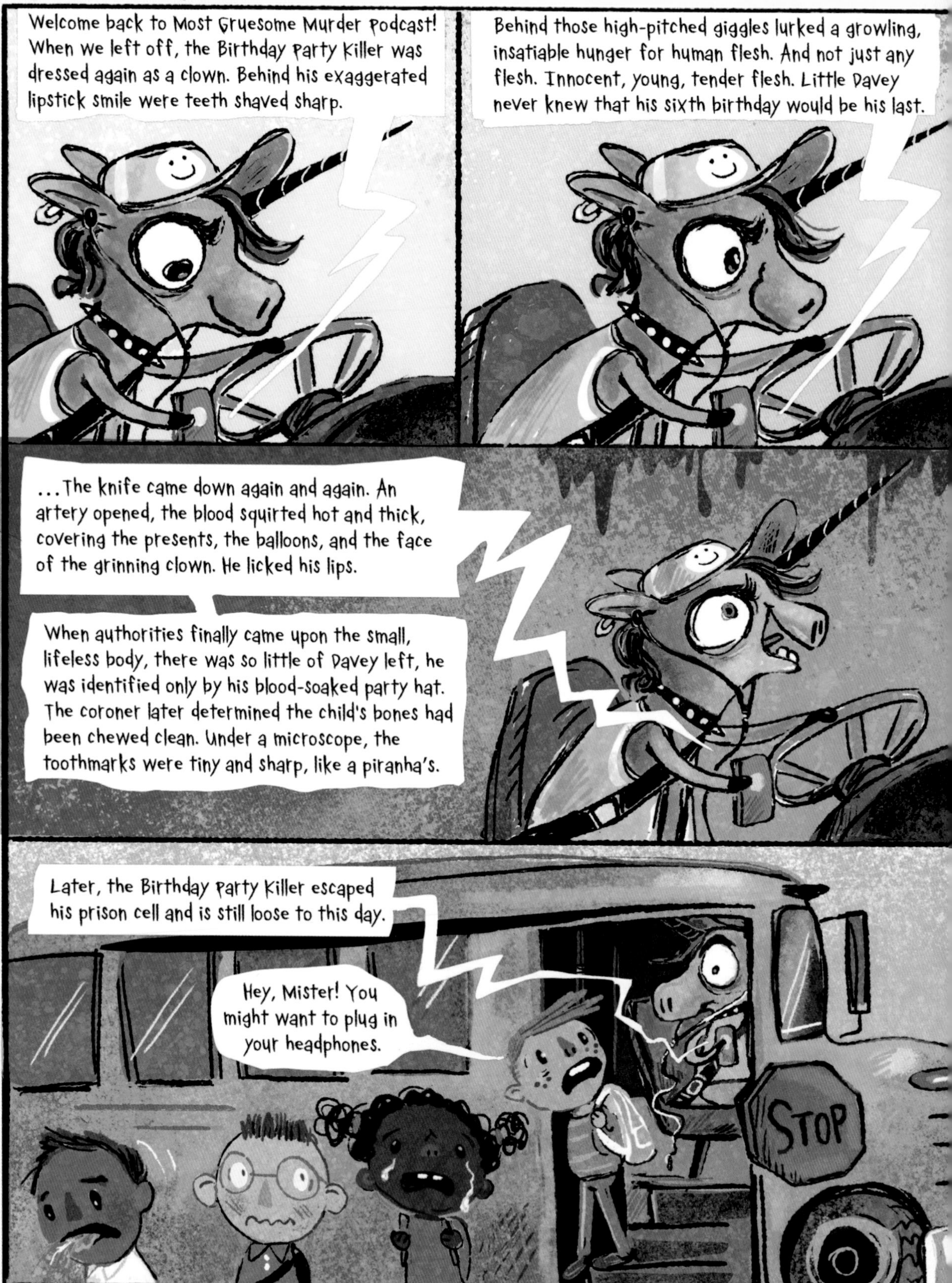
Welcome back to Most Gruesome Murder Podcast! When we left off, the Birthday Party Killer was dressed again as a clown. Behind his exaggerated lipstick smile were teeth shaved sharp.
Behind those high-pitched giggles lurked a growling, insatiable hunger for human flesh. And not just any flesh. Innocent, young, tender flesh. Little Davey never knew that his sixth birthday would be his last.
...The knife came down again and again. An artery opened, the blood squirted hot and thick, covering the presents, the balloons, and the face of the grinning clown. He licked his lips.
When authorities finally came upon the small, lifeless body, there was so little of Davey left, he was identified only by his blood-soaked party hat. The coroner later determined the child's bones had been chewed clean. Under a microscope, the toothmarks were tiny and sharp, like a piranha's.
Later, the Birthday Party Killer escaped his prison cell and is still loose to this day.
Hey, Mister! You might want to plug in your headphones.
STOP

STAB-O-WEEN

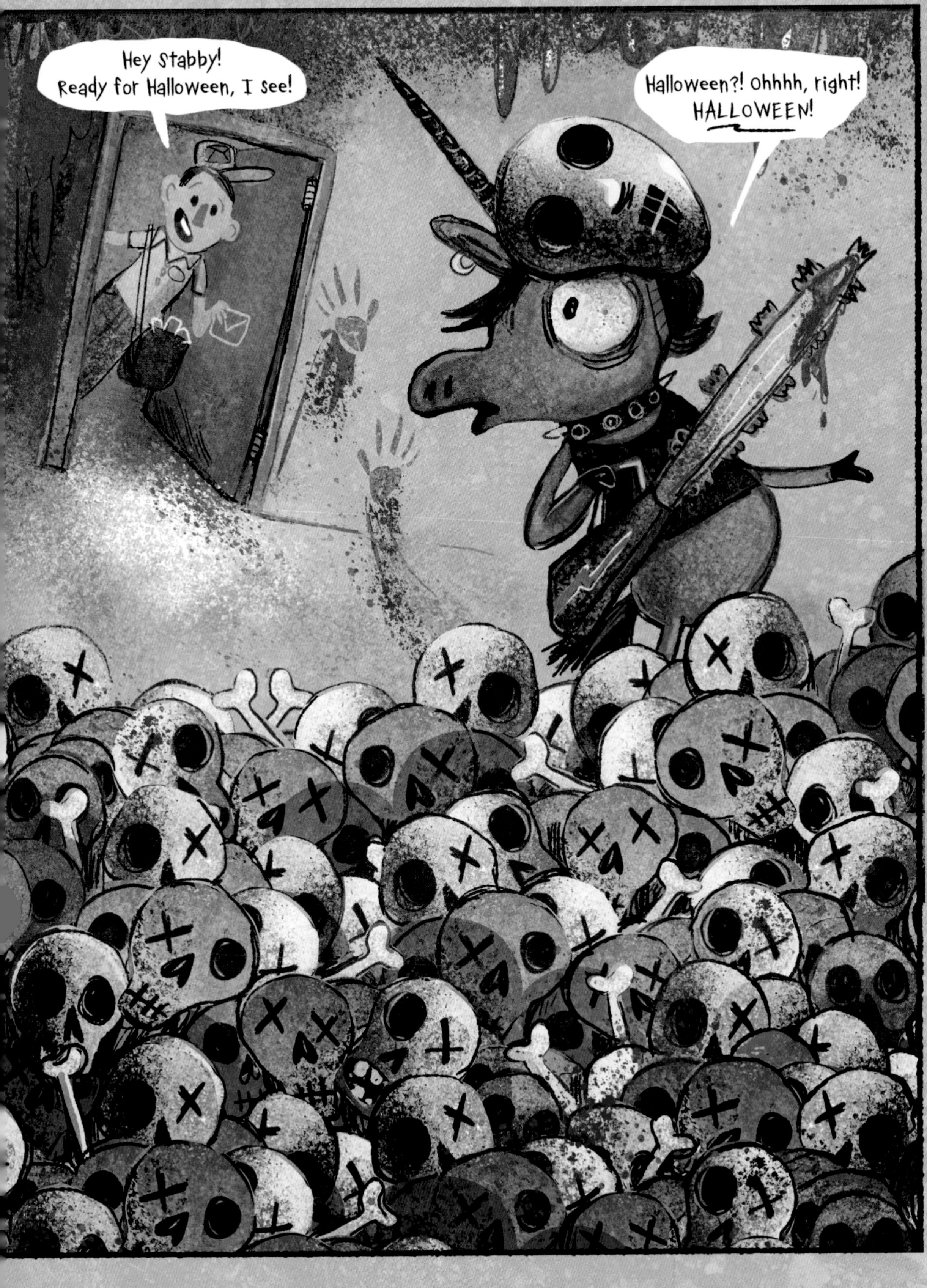
Hey Stabby!
Ready for Halloween, I see!
Halloween?! Ohhhh, right! HALLOWEEN!

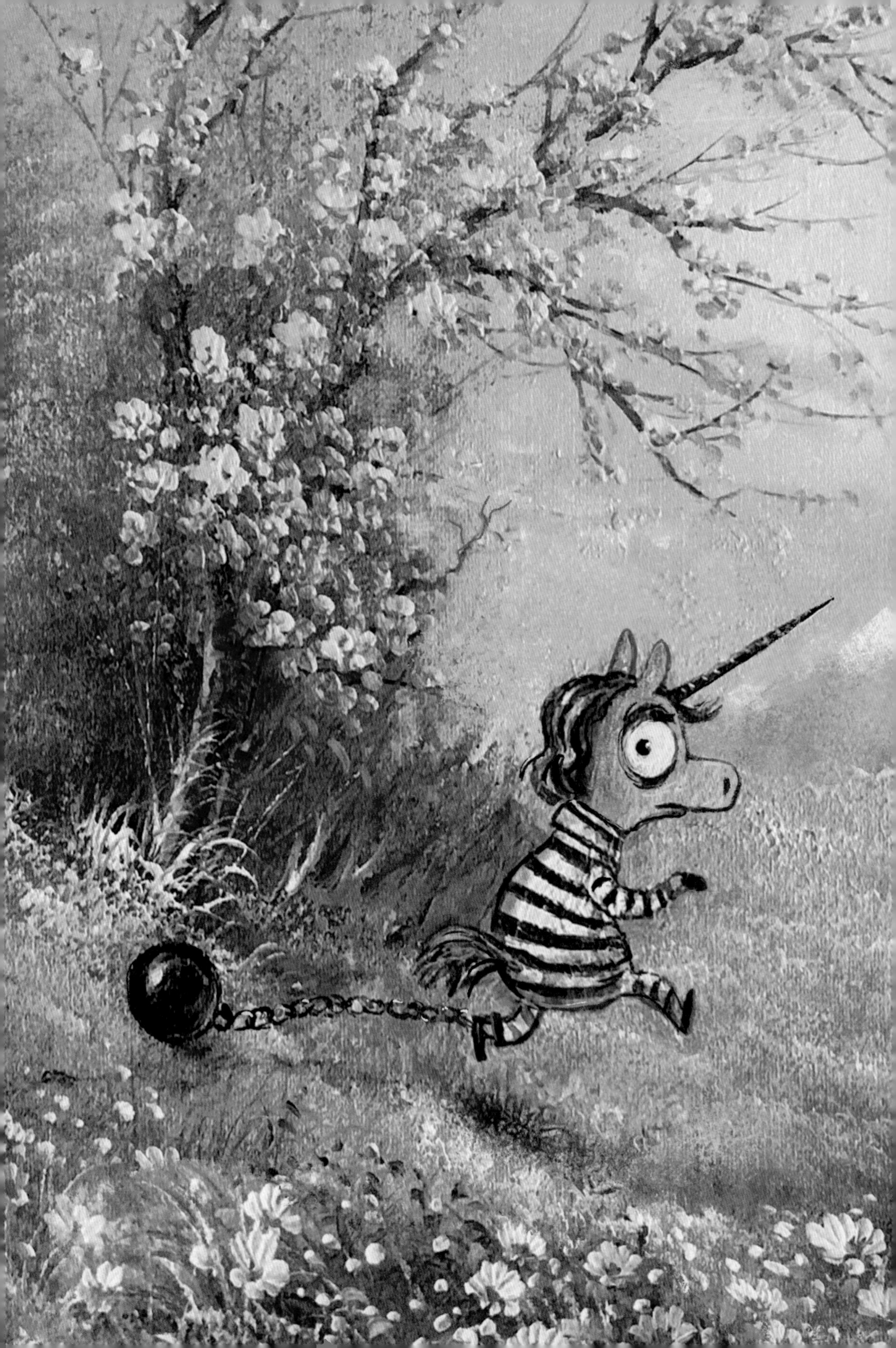

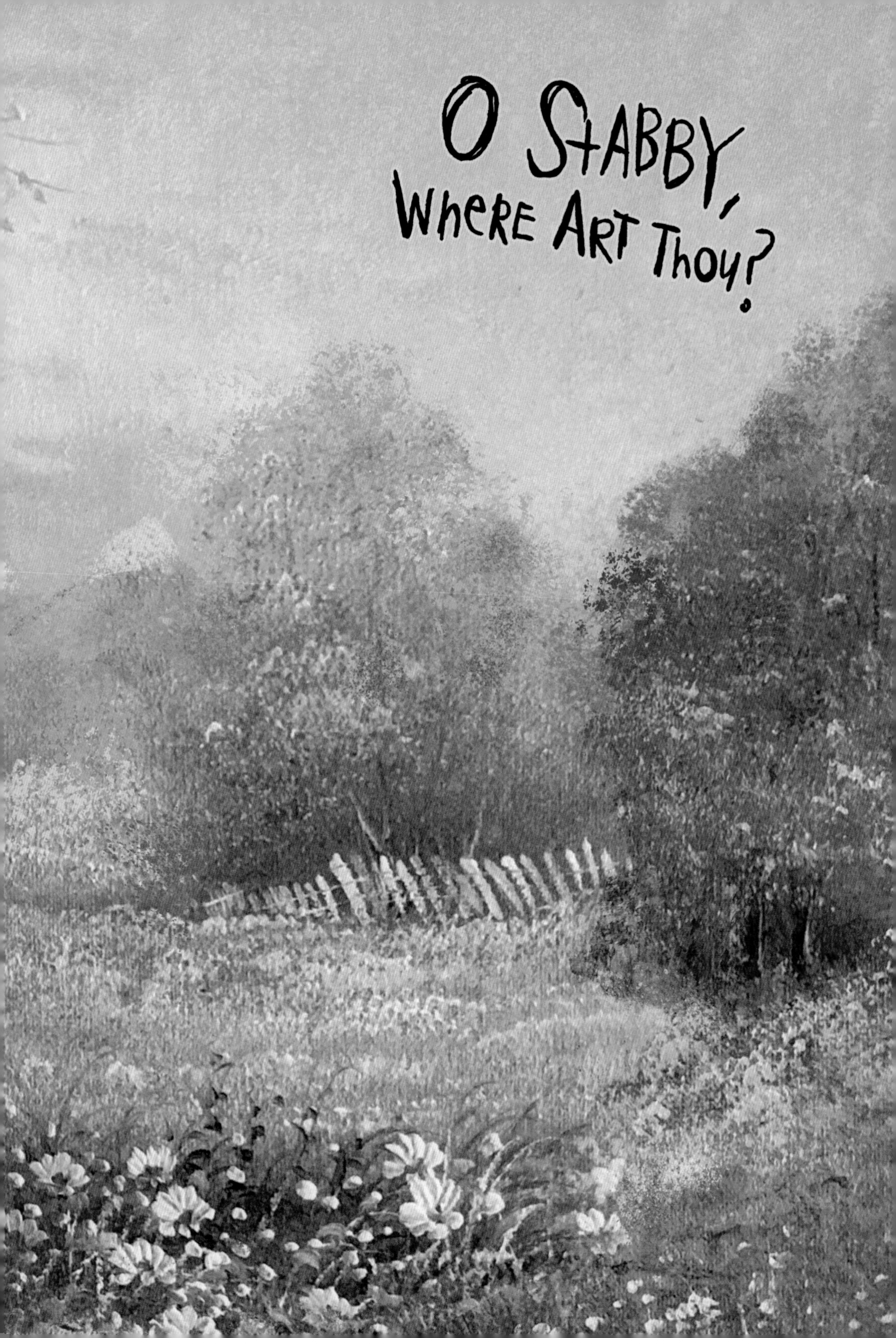
O STABBY,
WHERE ART THOU?

Pets

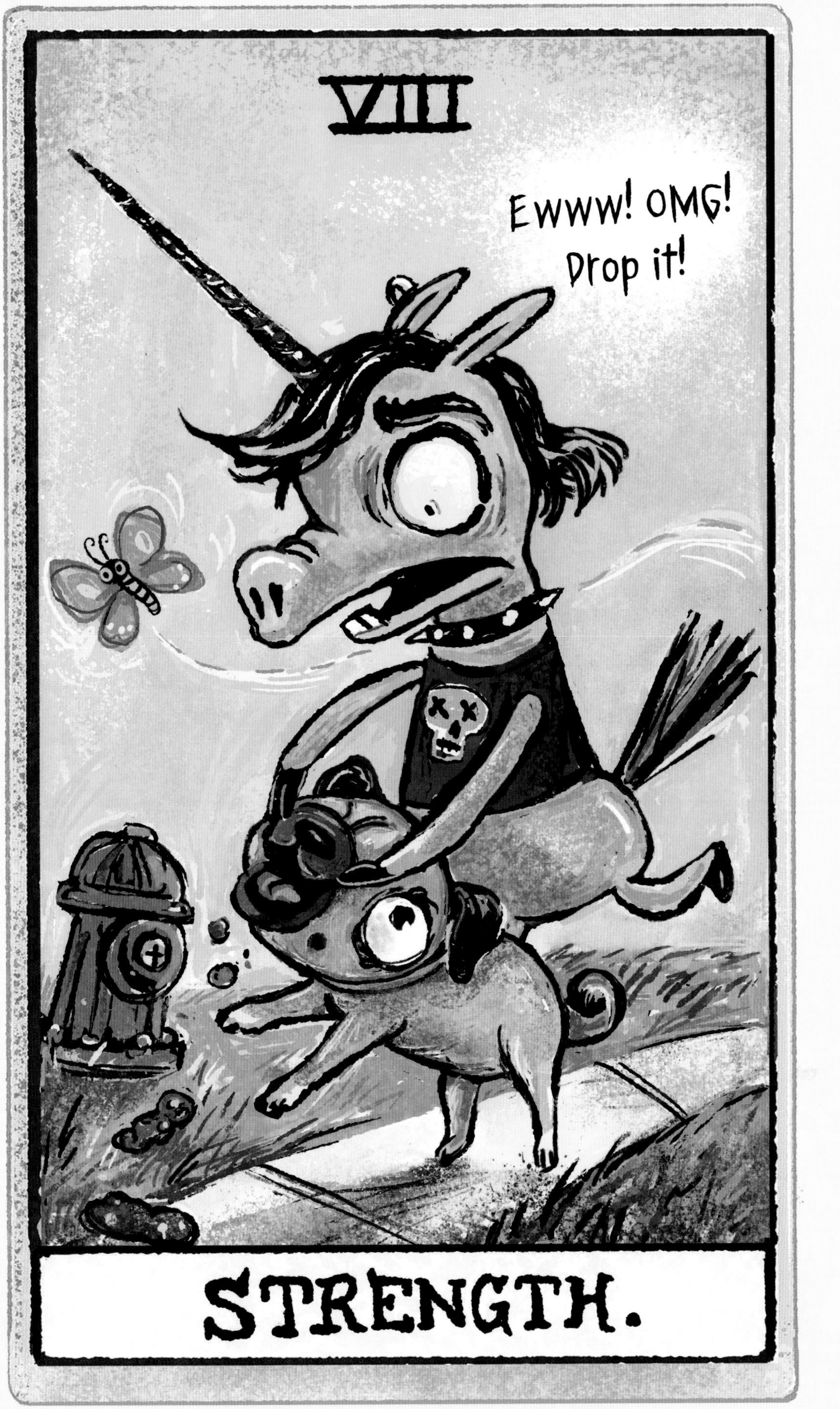
VIII
Ewww! OMG!
Drop it!
STRENGTH.

Pet Shop

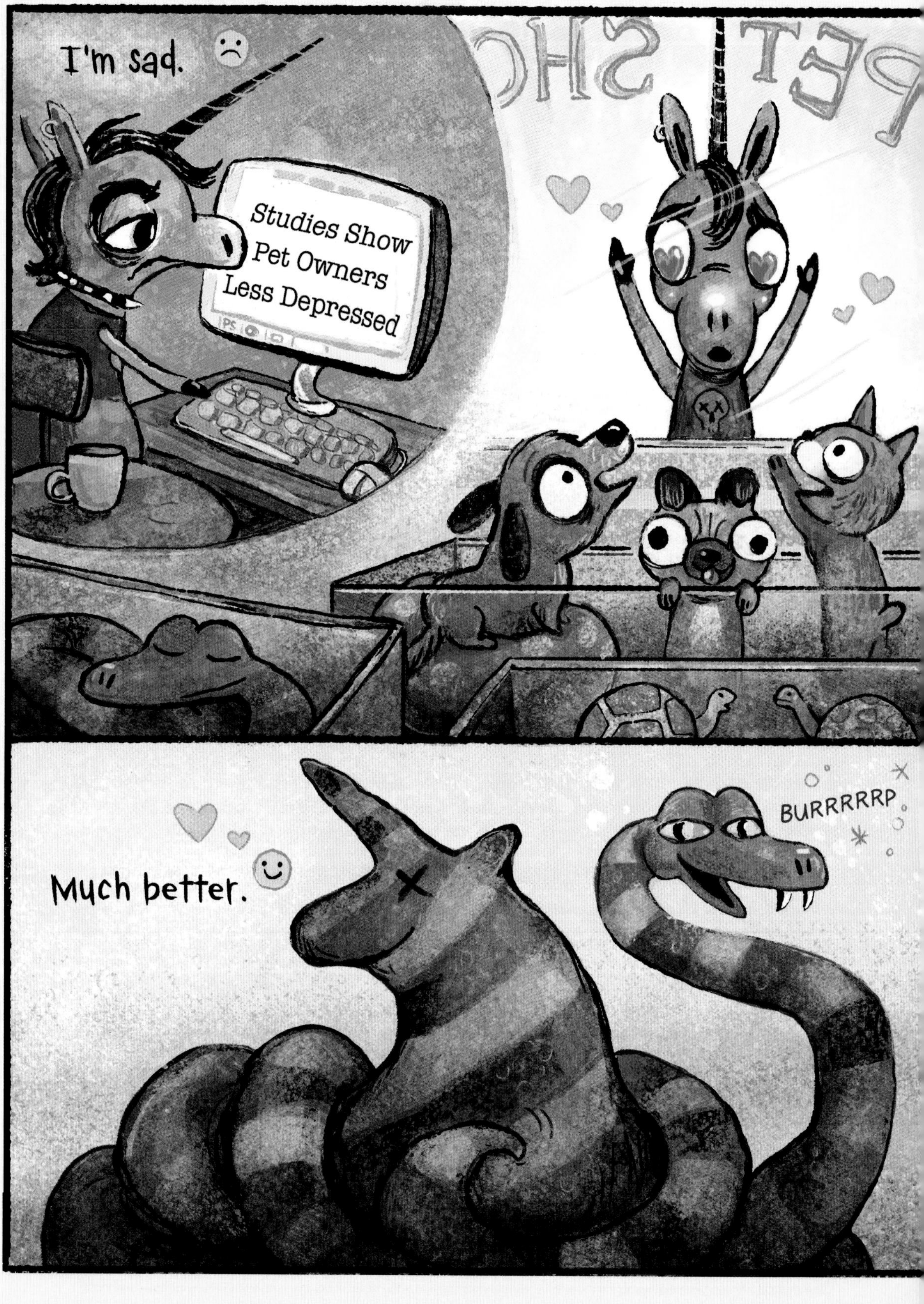
I'm sad.
Studies Show
Pet Owners
Less Depressed
PET SHO
Much better.
BURRRRRP

Friendly

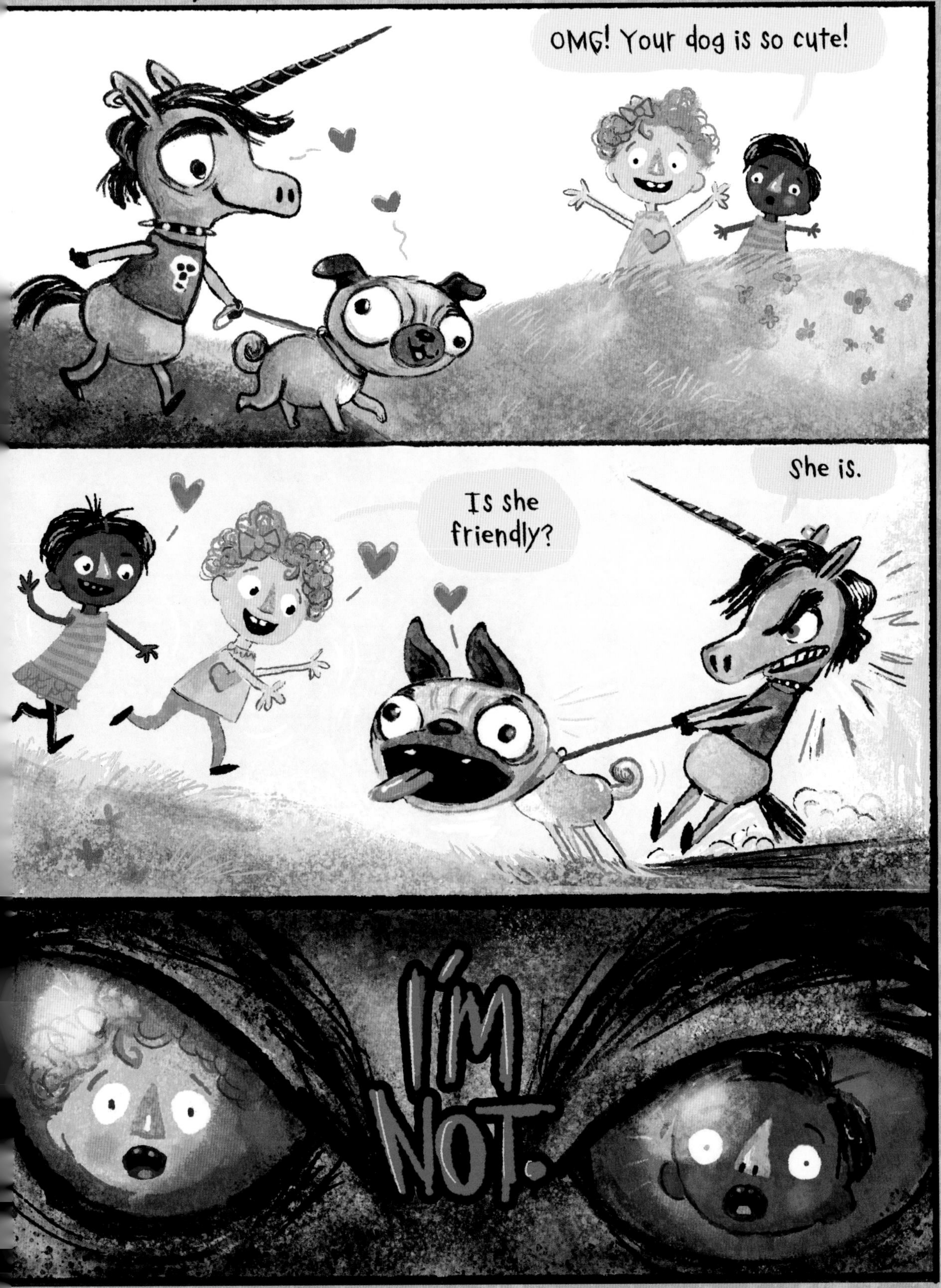
OMG! Your dog is so cute!
Is she friendly?
She is.
I'M NOT.

Love & FAMiLY

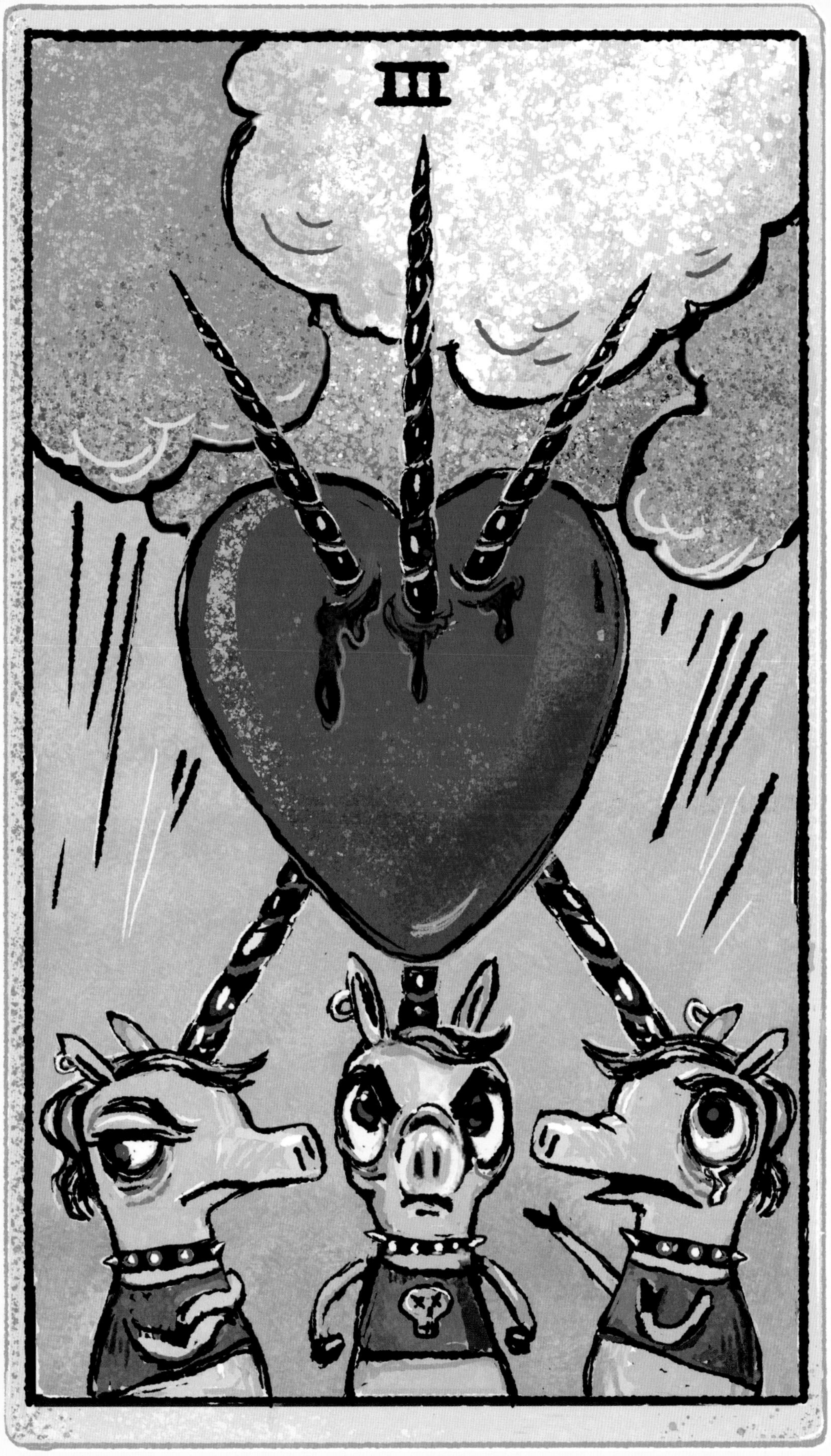
III

CUPID

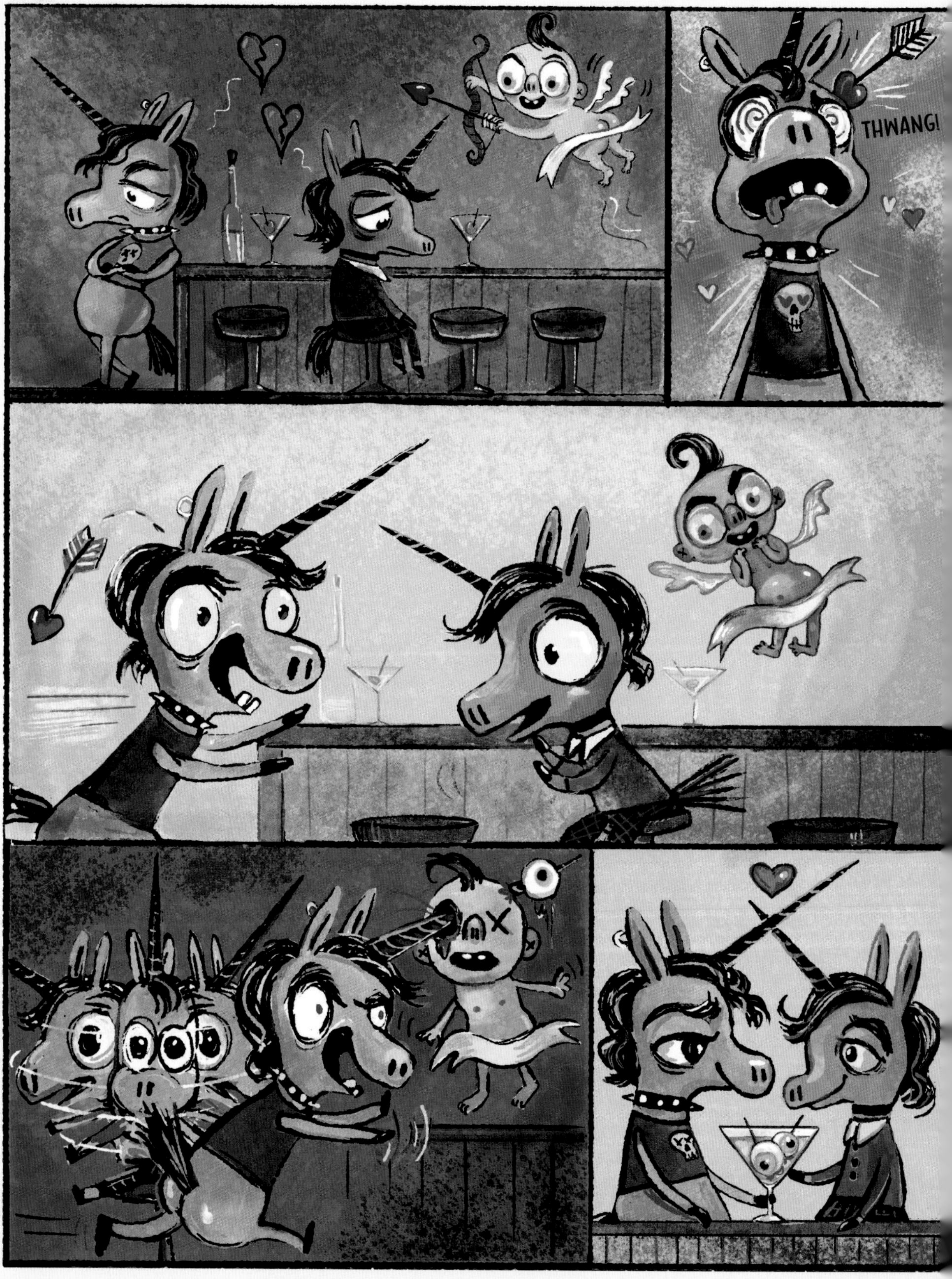
THWANG!

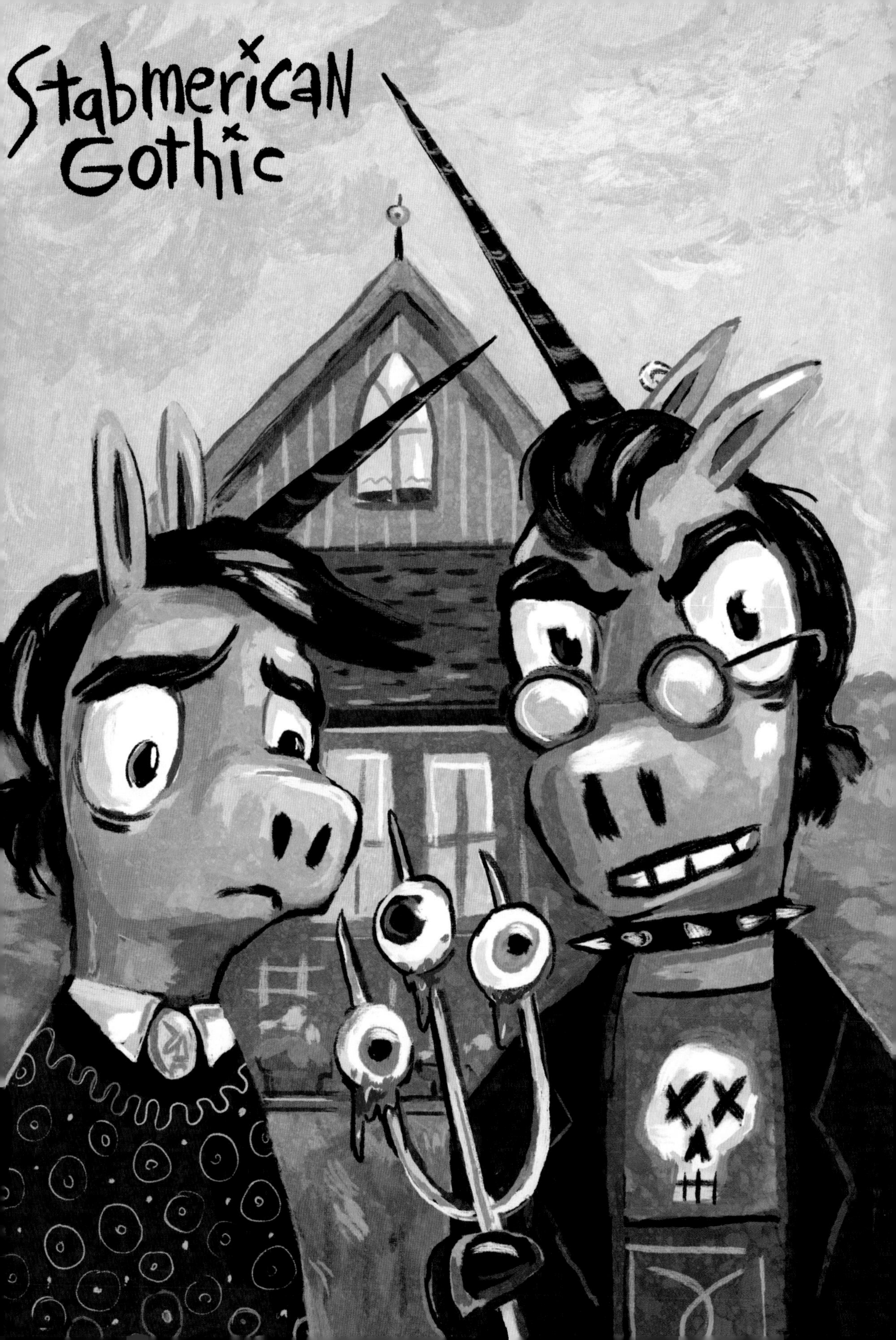
Stabmerican Gothic

Parent Trap

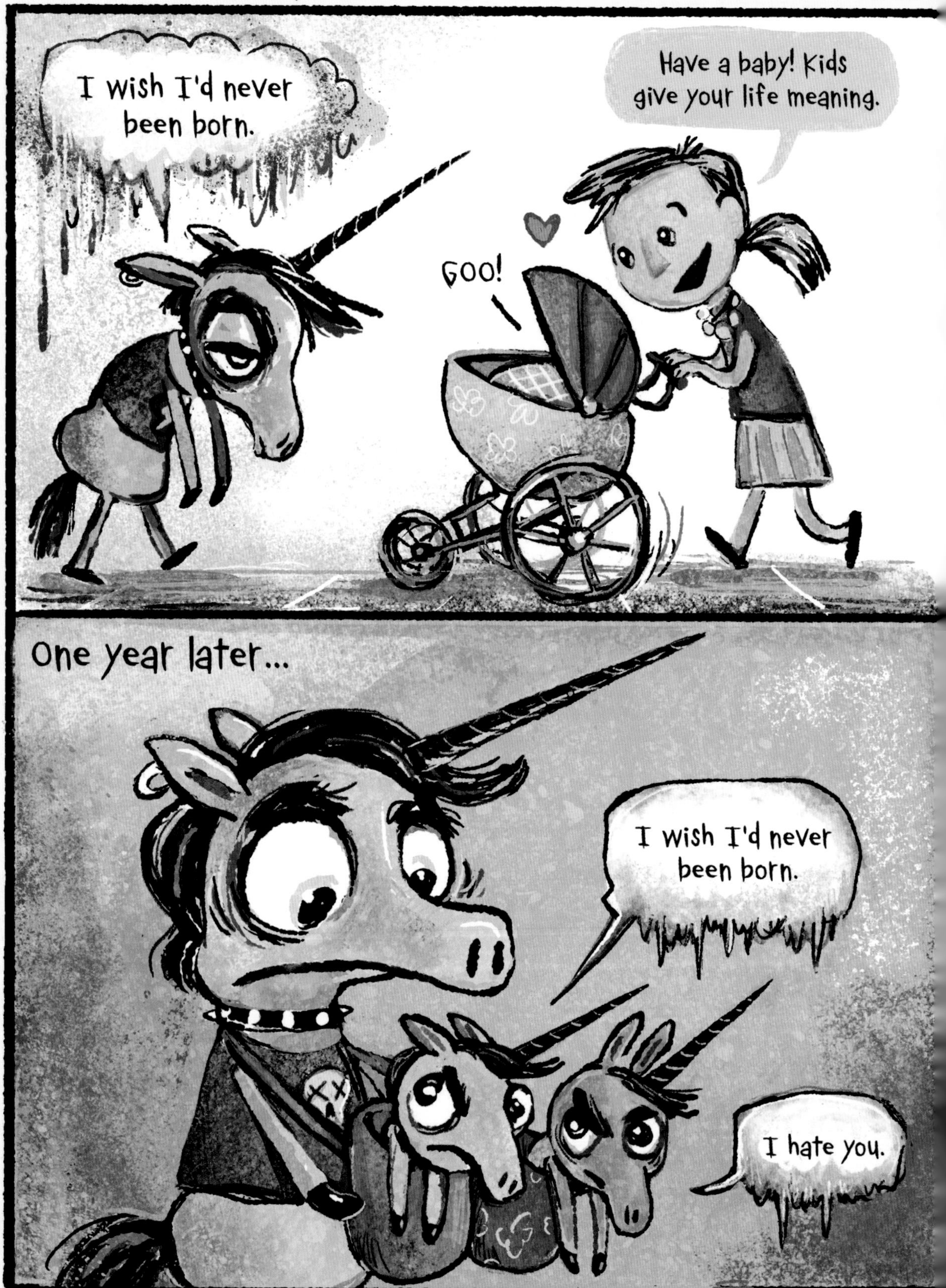
I wish I'd never been born.
Have a baby! Kids give your life meaning.
GOO!
One year later...
I wish I'd never been born.
I hate you.

Lawn Darts

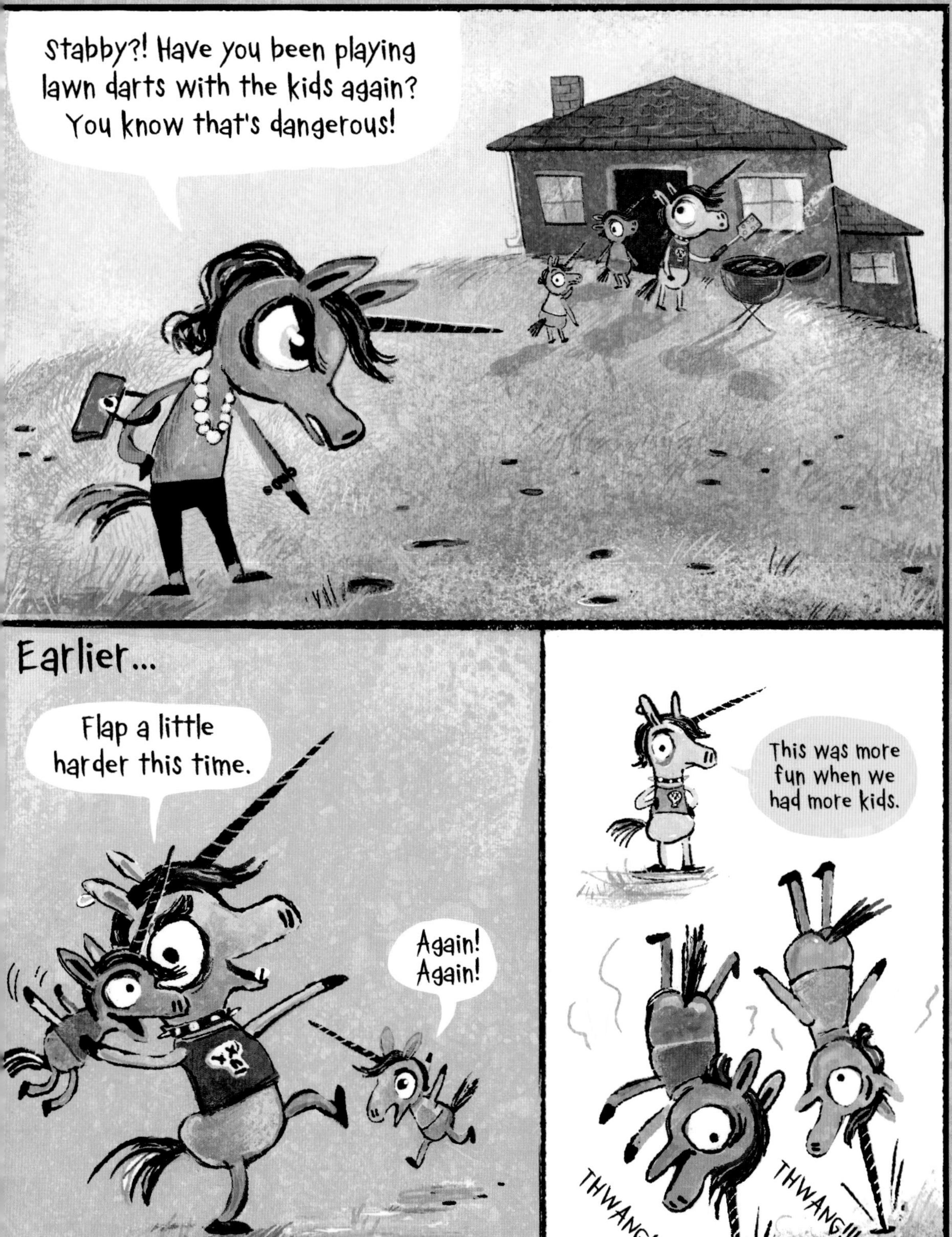

Stabby?! Have you been playing lawn darts with the kids again? You know that's dangerous!
Earlier...
Flap a little harder this time.
Again! Again!
This was more fun when we had more kids.
THWANG!!!
THWANG!!!

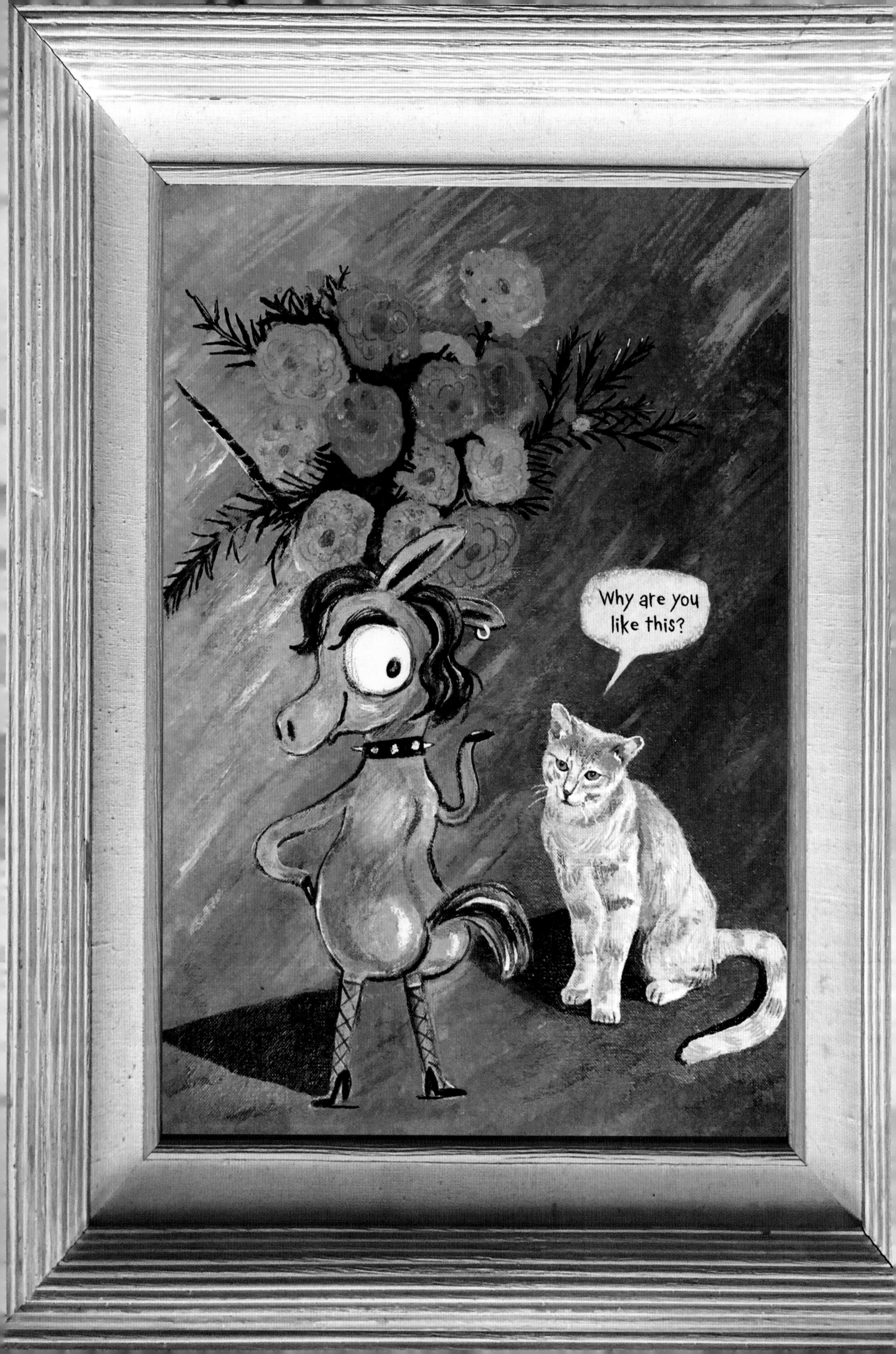
Why are you like this?

Zoocorns

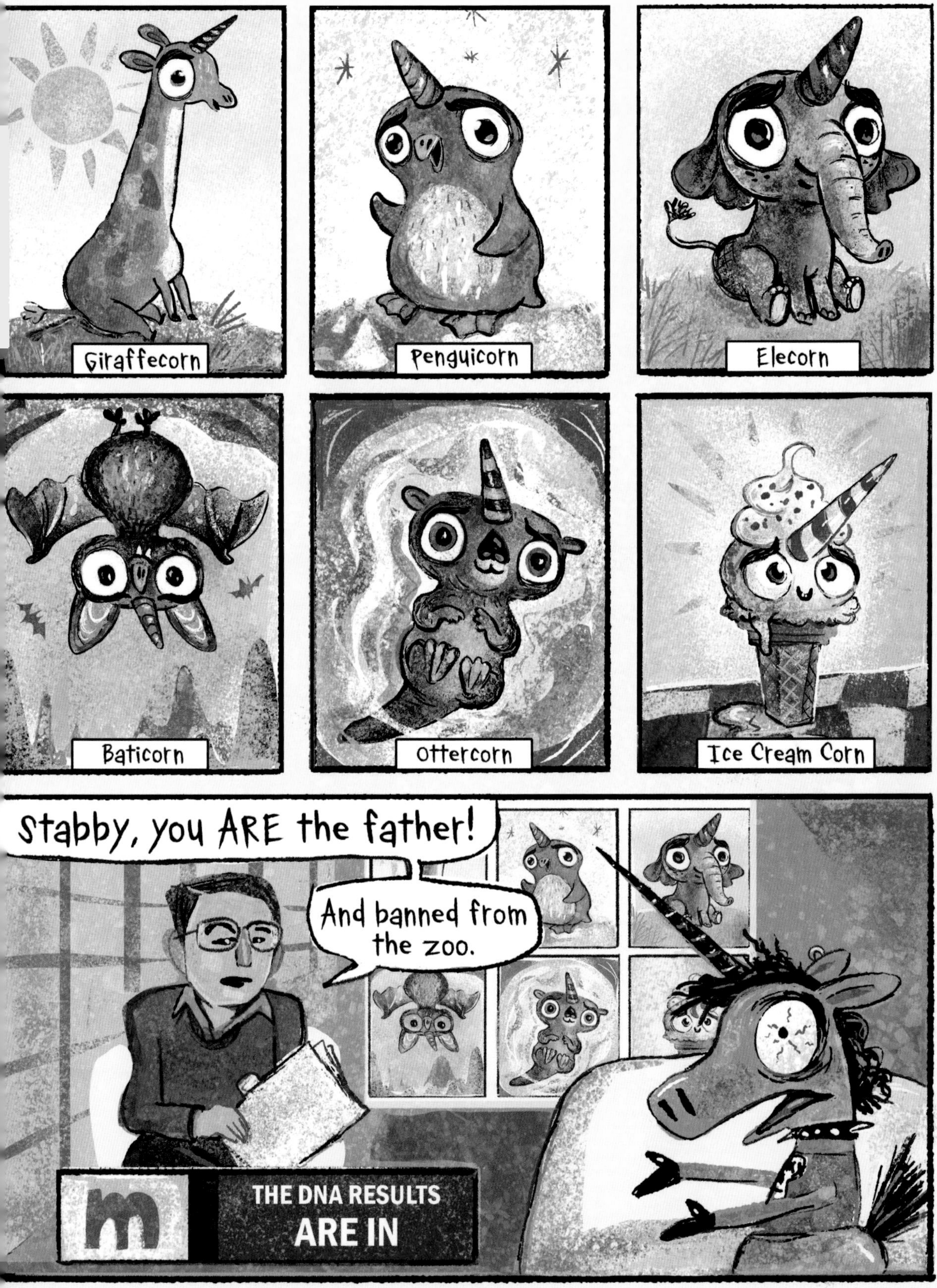
Giraffecorn
Penguicorn
Elecorn
Baticorn
Ottercorn
Ice Cream Corn
Stabby, you ARE the father!
And banned from the zoo.
THE DNA RESULTS ARE IN

INTROVERTING

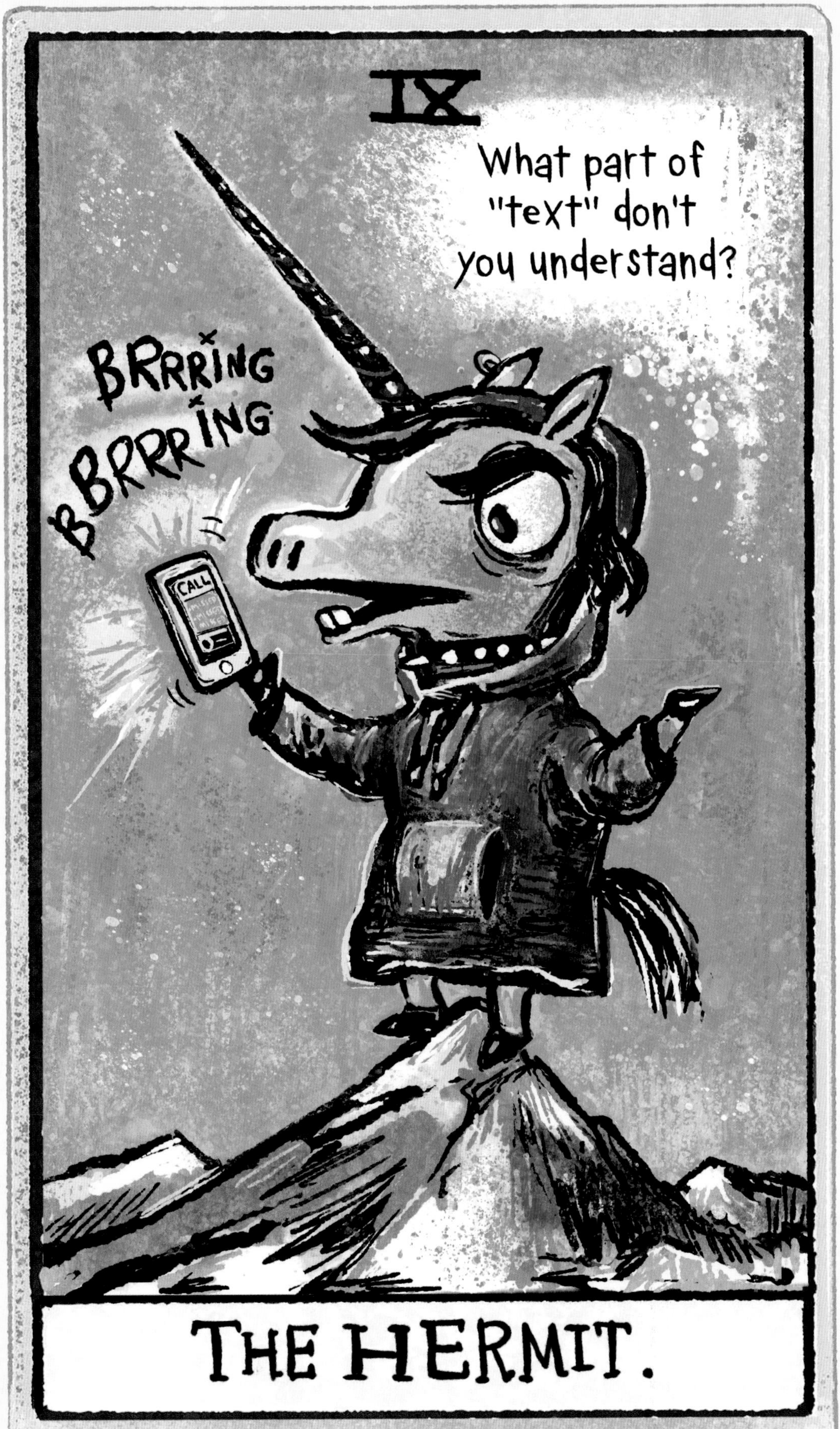
IX
What part of "text" don't you understand?
BRRRING
BBRRRING
CALL
THE HERMIT.

Birthday

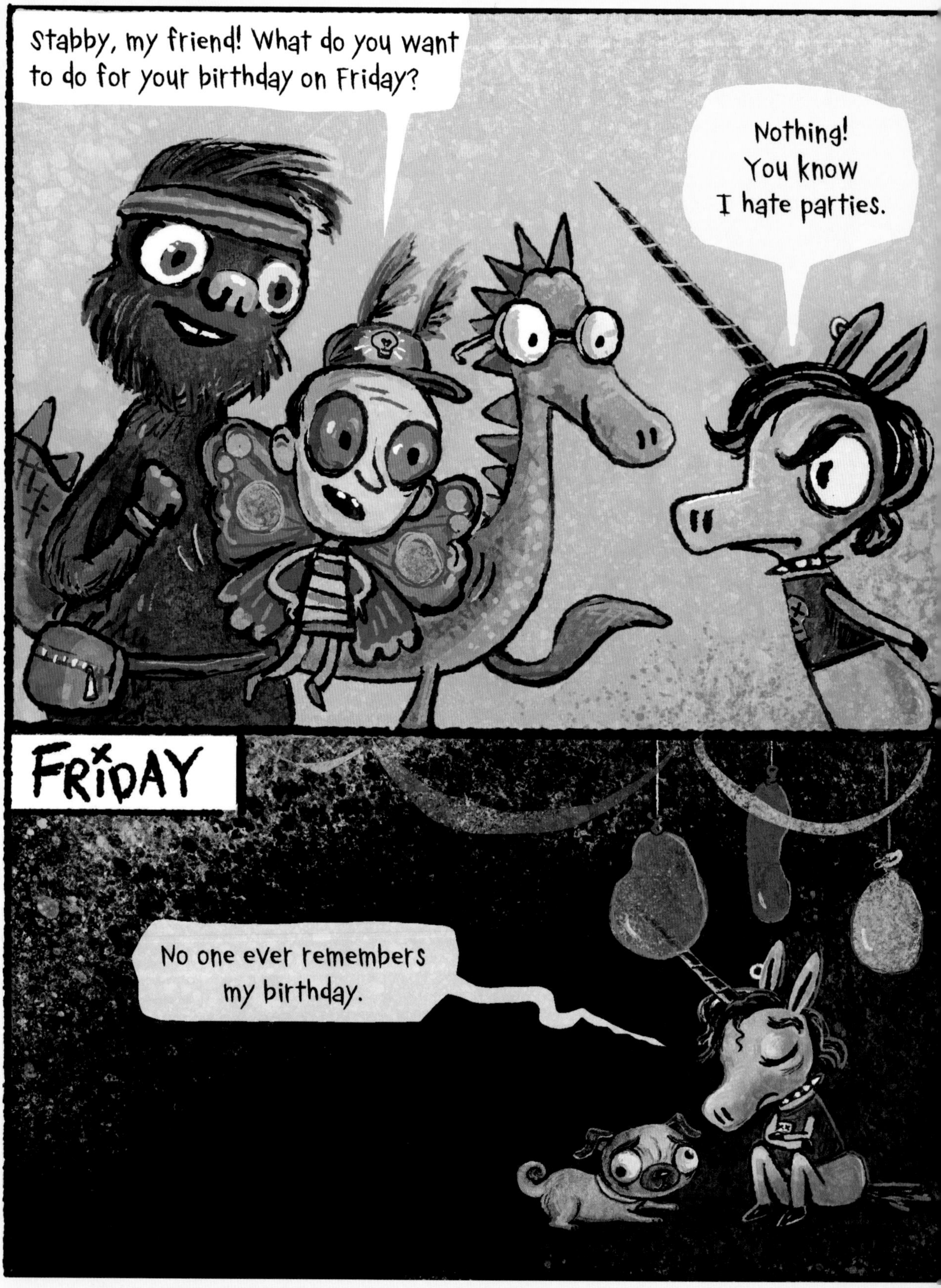

Stabby, my friend! What do you want to do for your birthday on Friday?
Nothing! You know I hate parties.
FRIDAY
No one ever remembers my birthday.

The Little Stabmaid

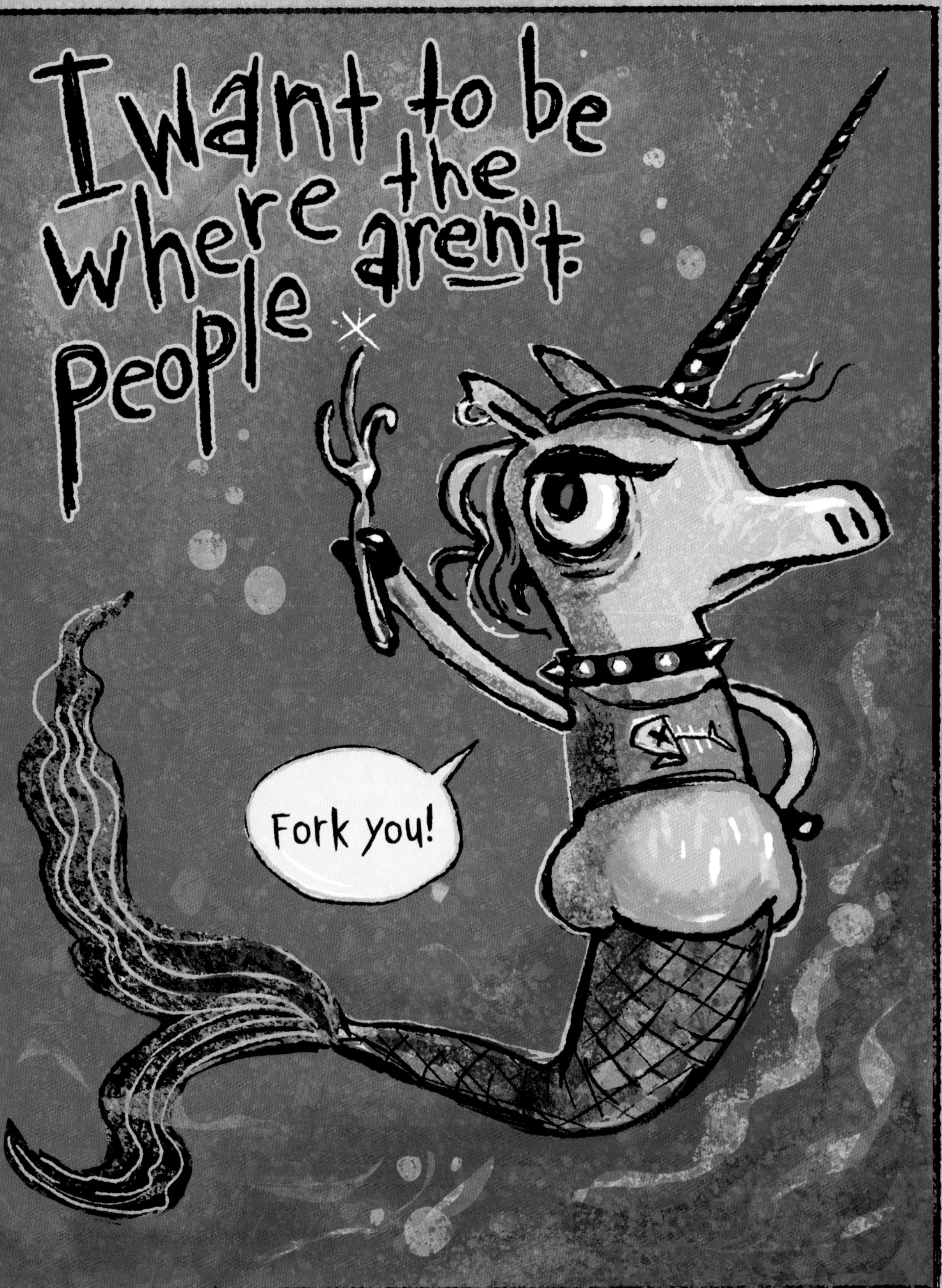
I want to be where the people aren't.
Fork you!

"Pants"

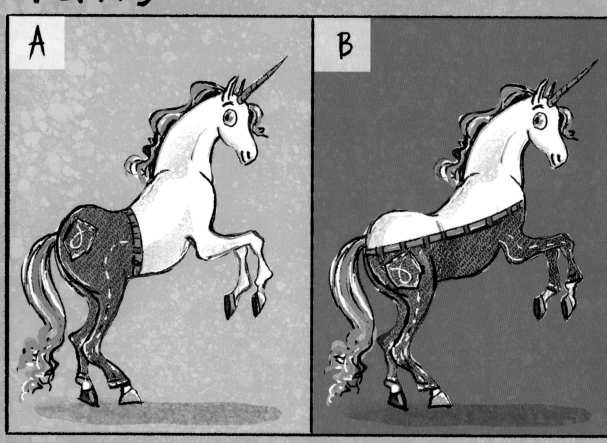

A

B

C

What pants?

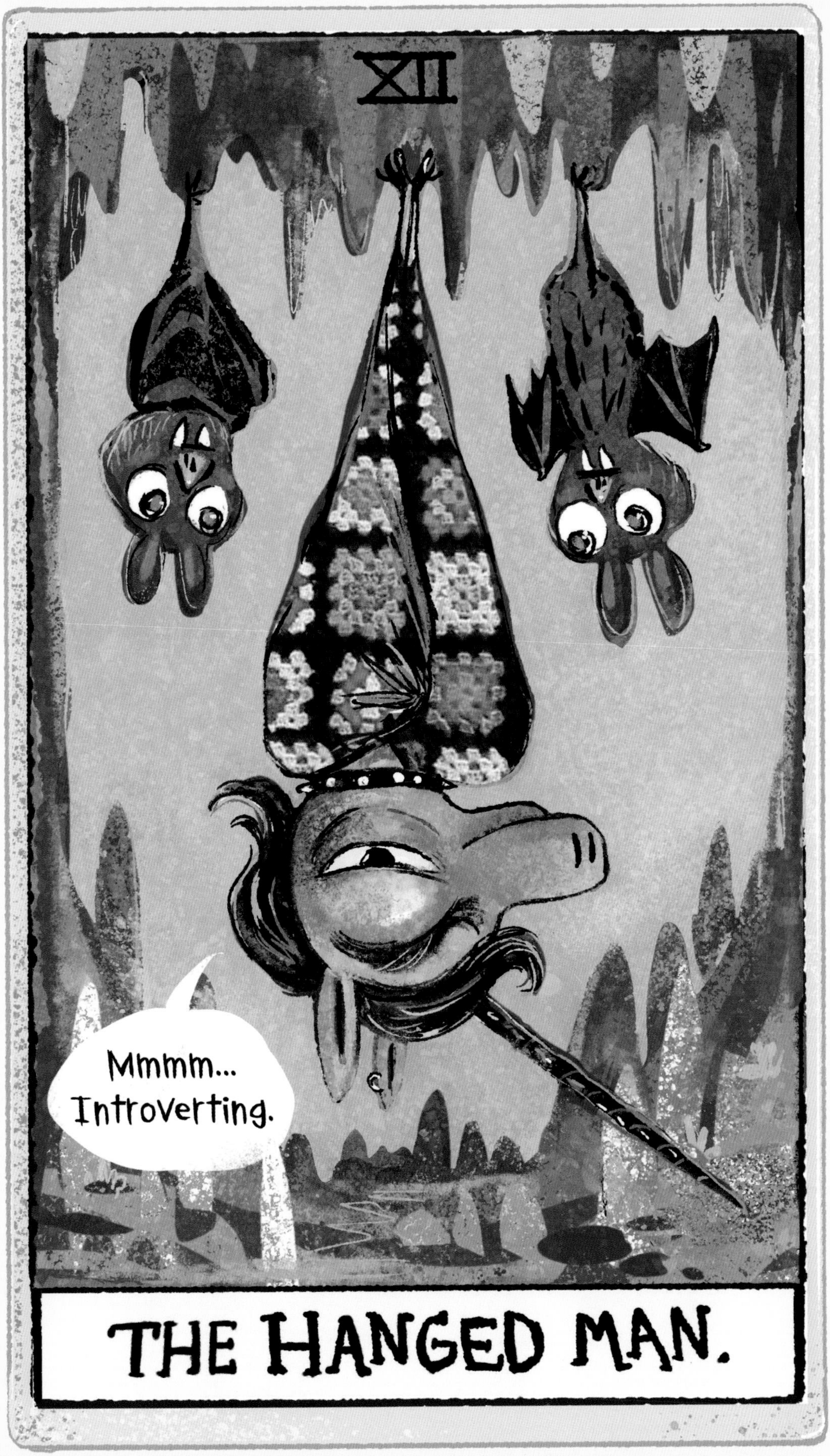
XII
Mmmm...
Introverting.
THE HANGED MAN.

Extra-Terrorestrial

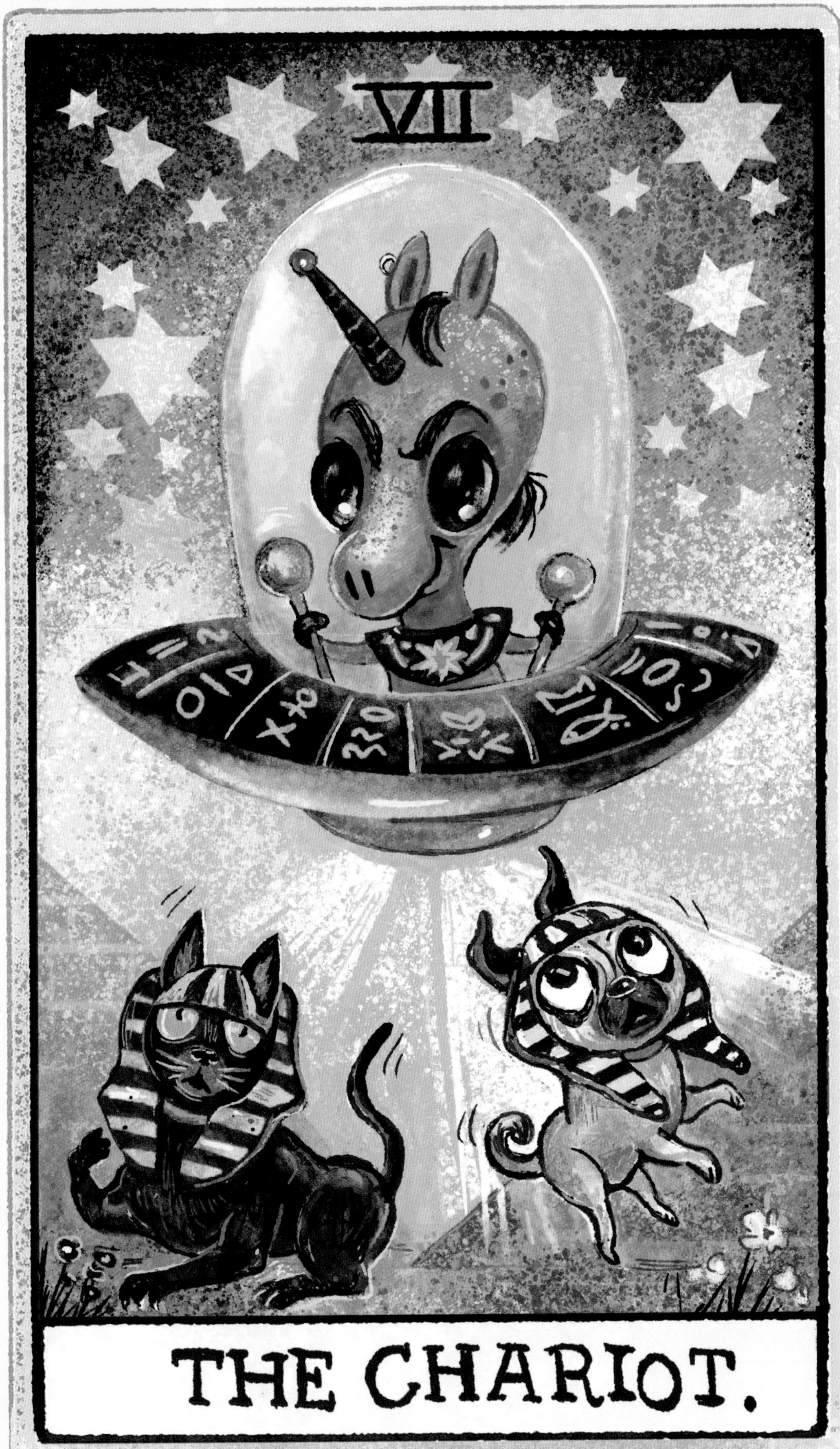
VII
THE CHARIOT.

E. Tease

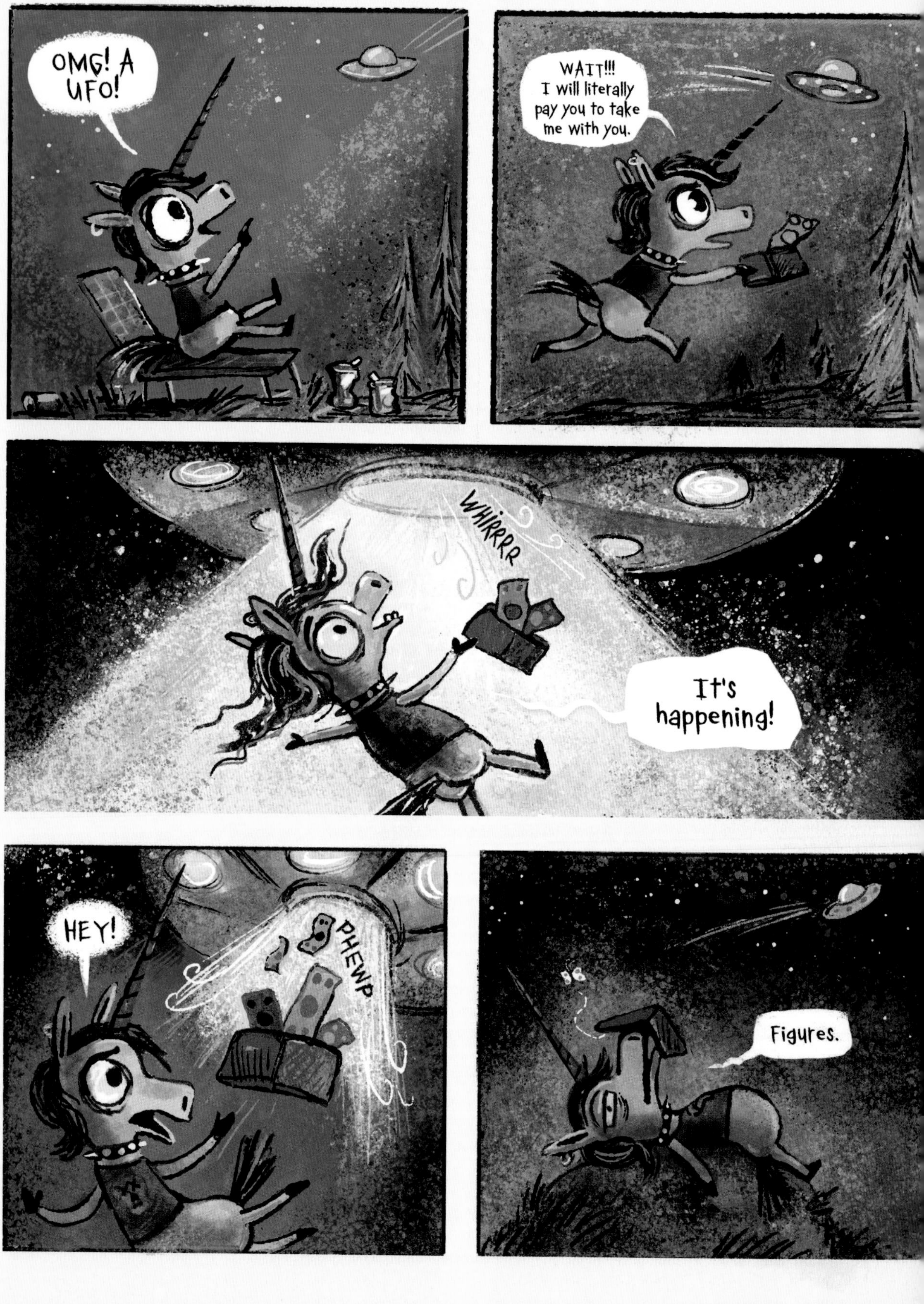

OMG! A UFO!
WAIT!!! I will literally pay you to take me with you.
WHIRRRR
It's happening!
HEY!
PHEWP
Figures.

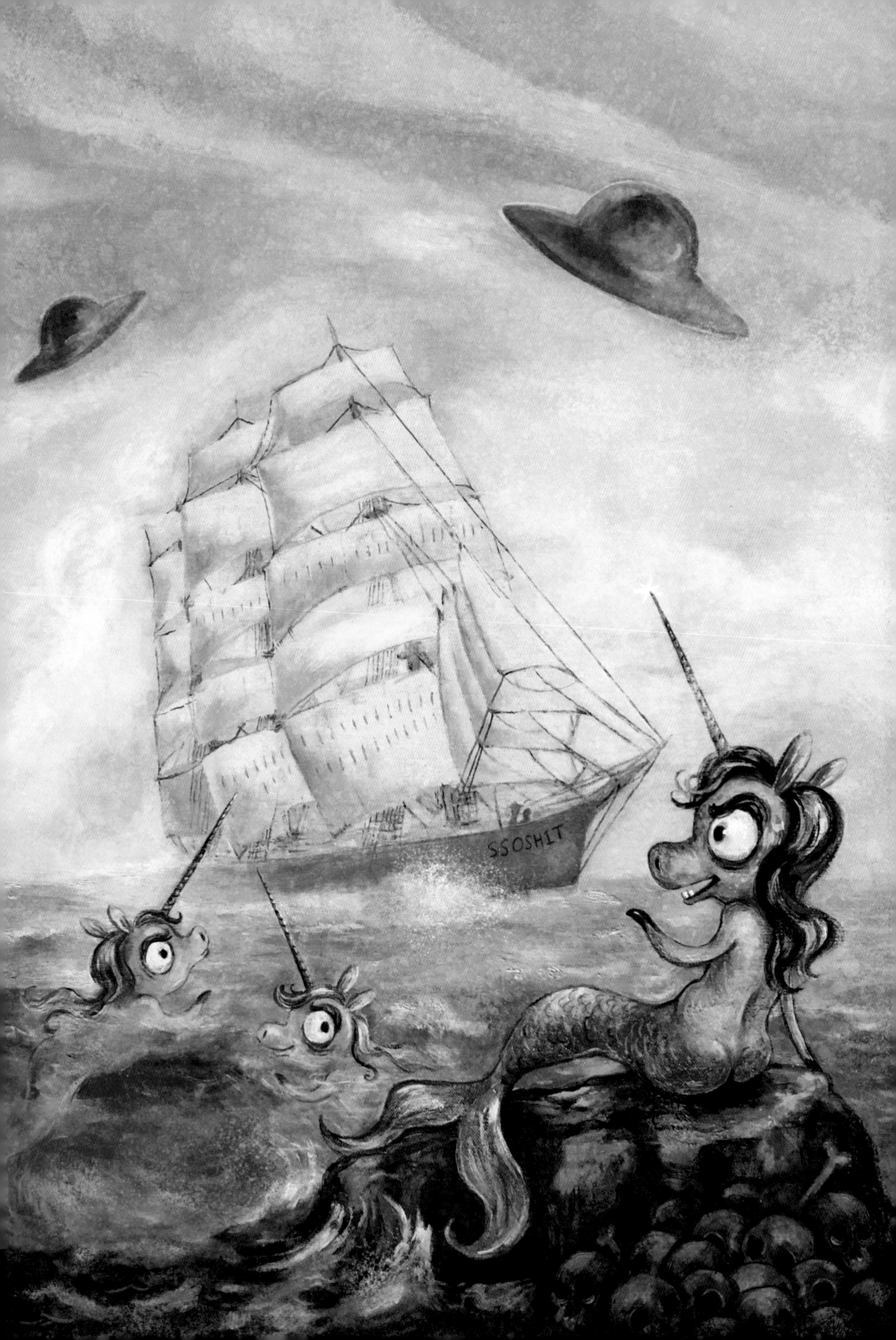
SSOSHIT

UnSocial MEDIA

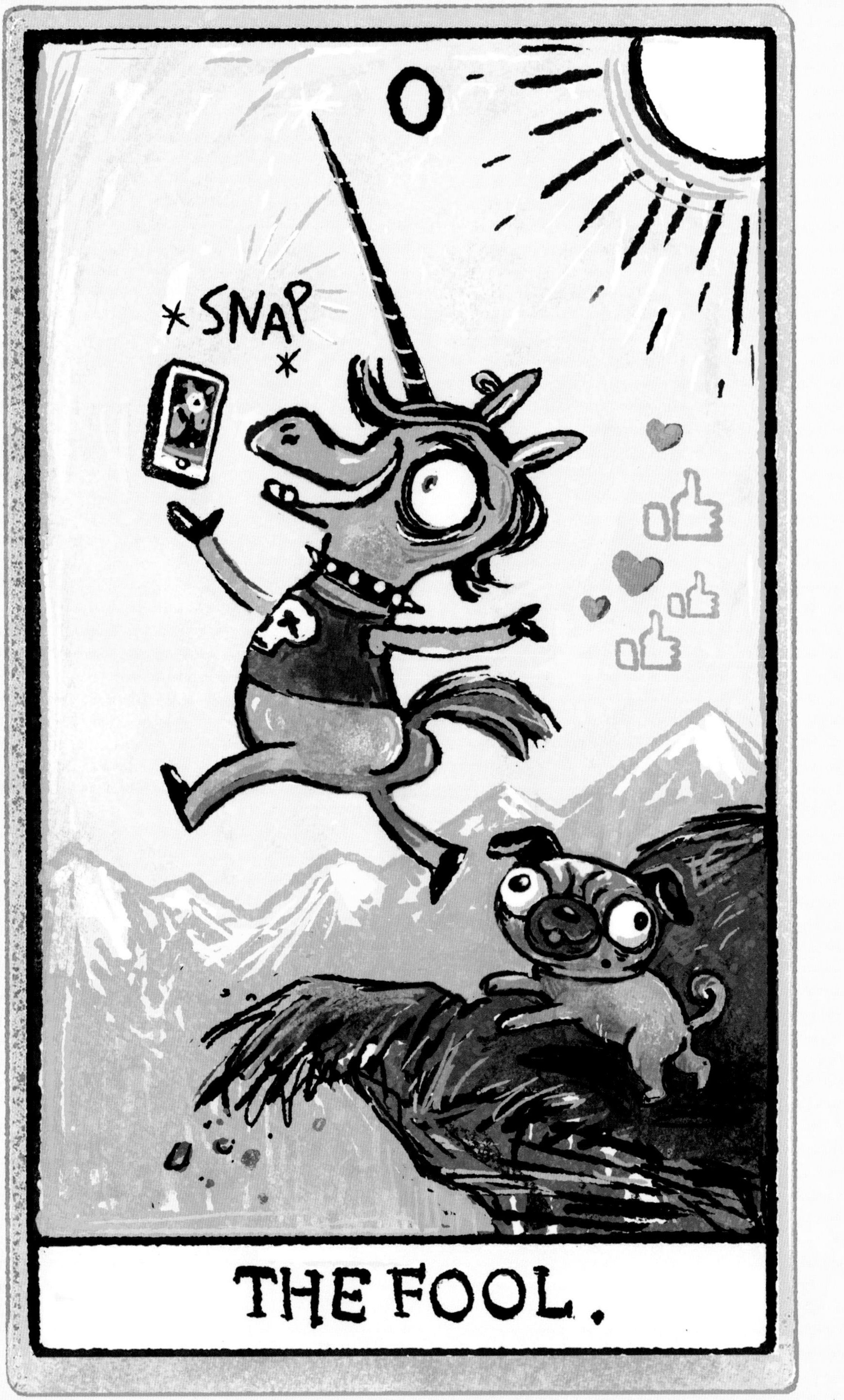
0
SNAP
THE FOOL.

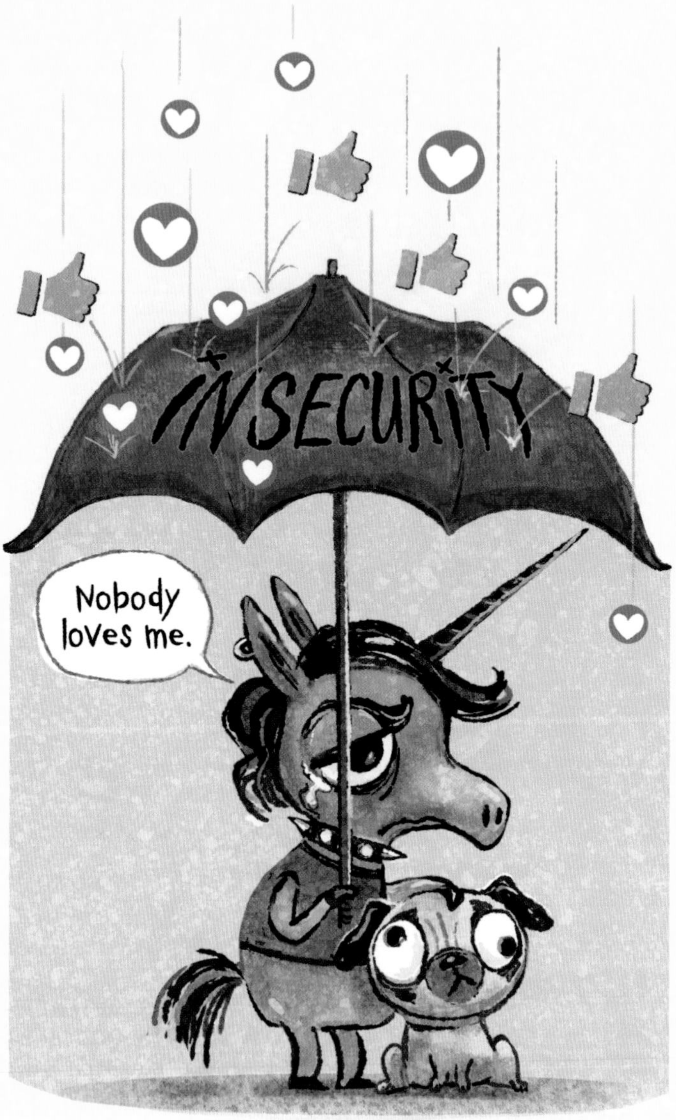
INSECURITY
Nobody loves me.

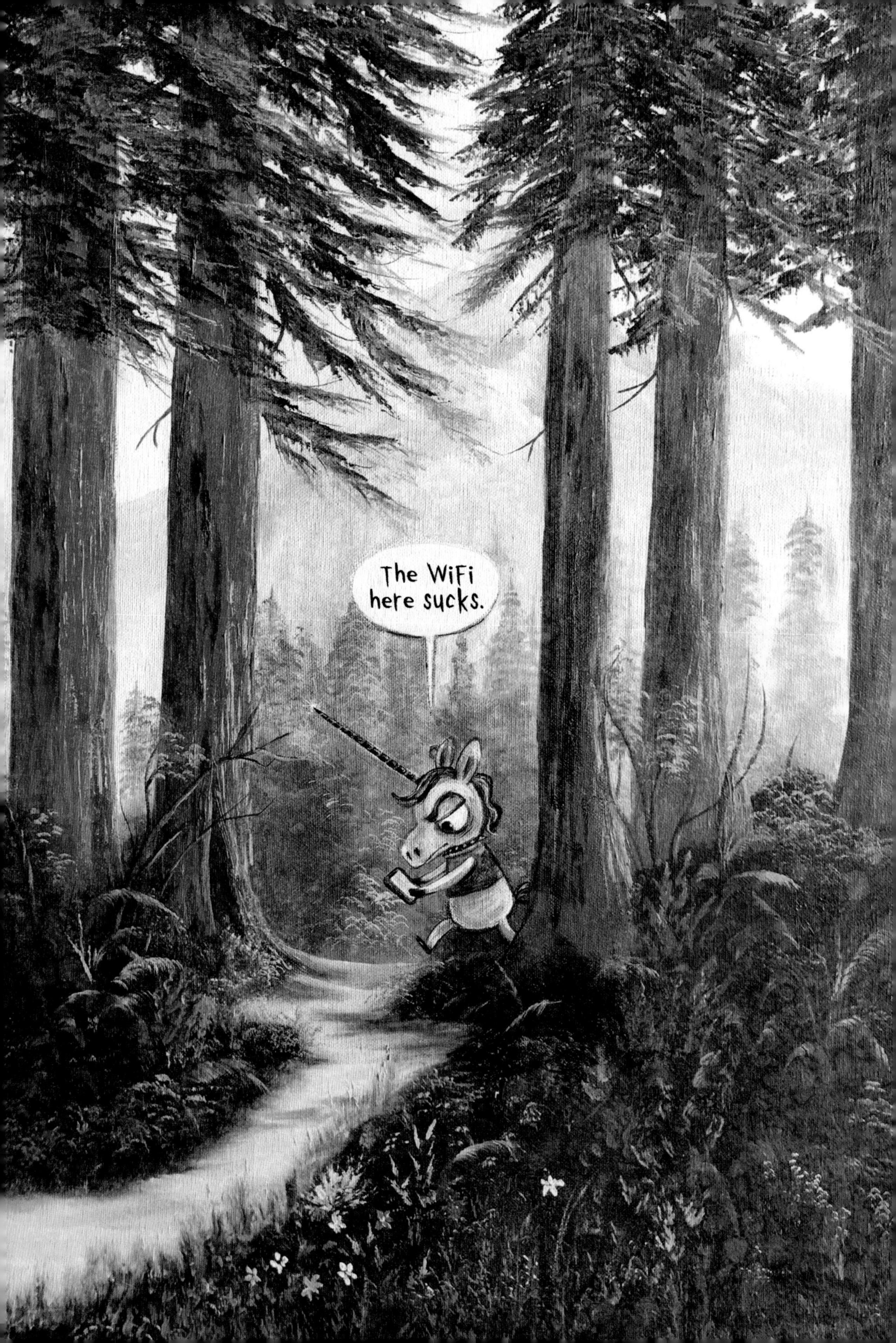
The WiFi here sucks.

PANDeMIC

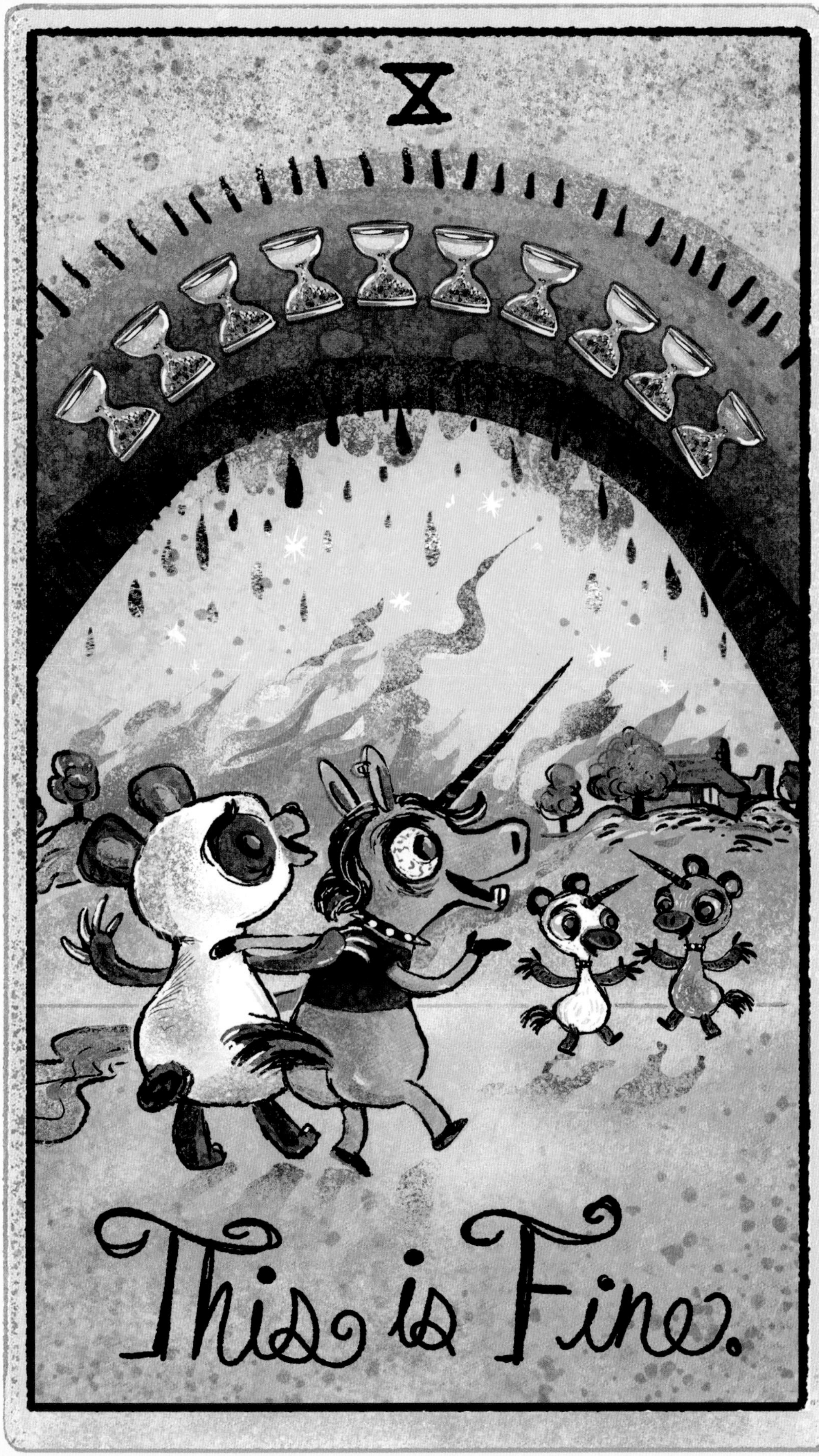

X
This is Fine.

Guest

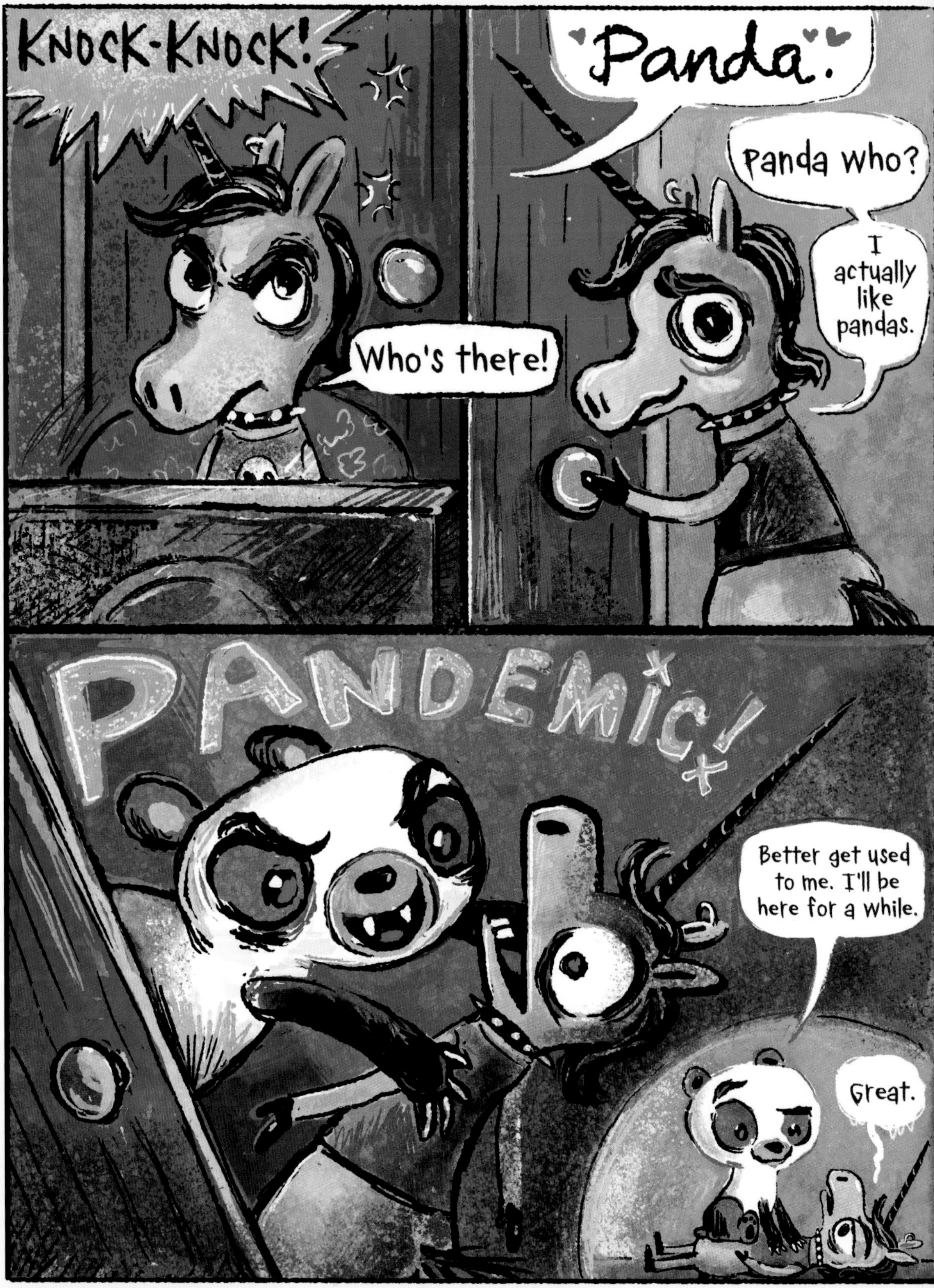

KNOCK-KNOCK!
Who's there!
Panda.
Panda who?
I actually like pandas.
PANDEMIC!
Better get used to me. I'll be here for a while.
Great.

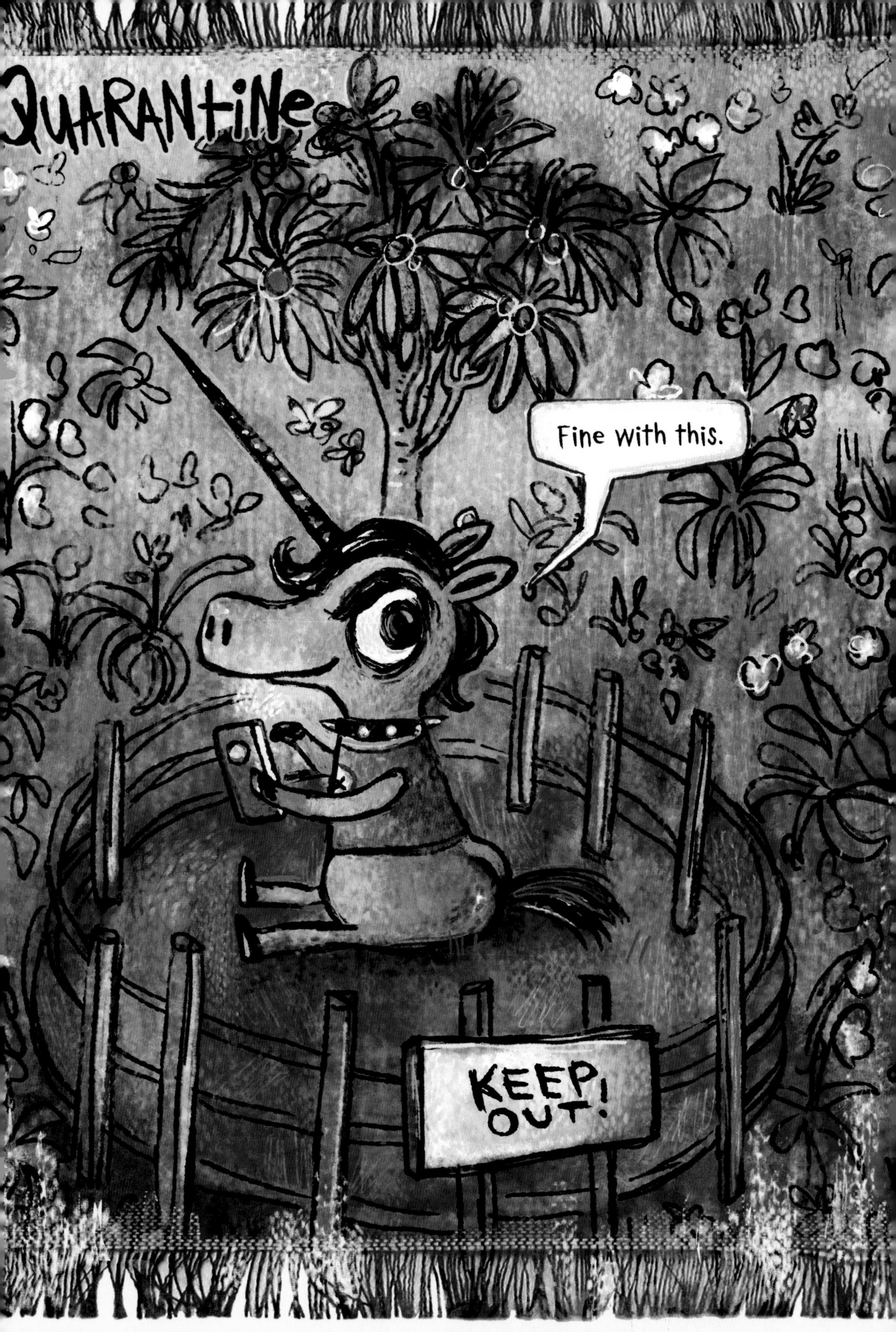
QUARANTINE
Fine with this.
KEEP OUT!

PLATES

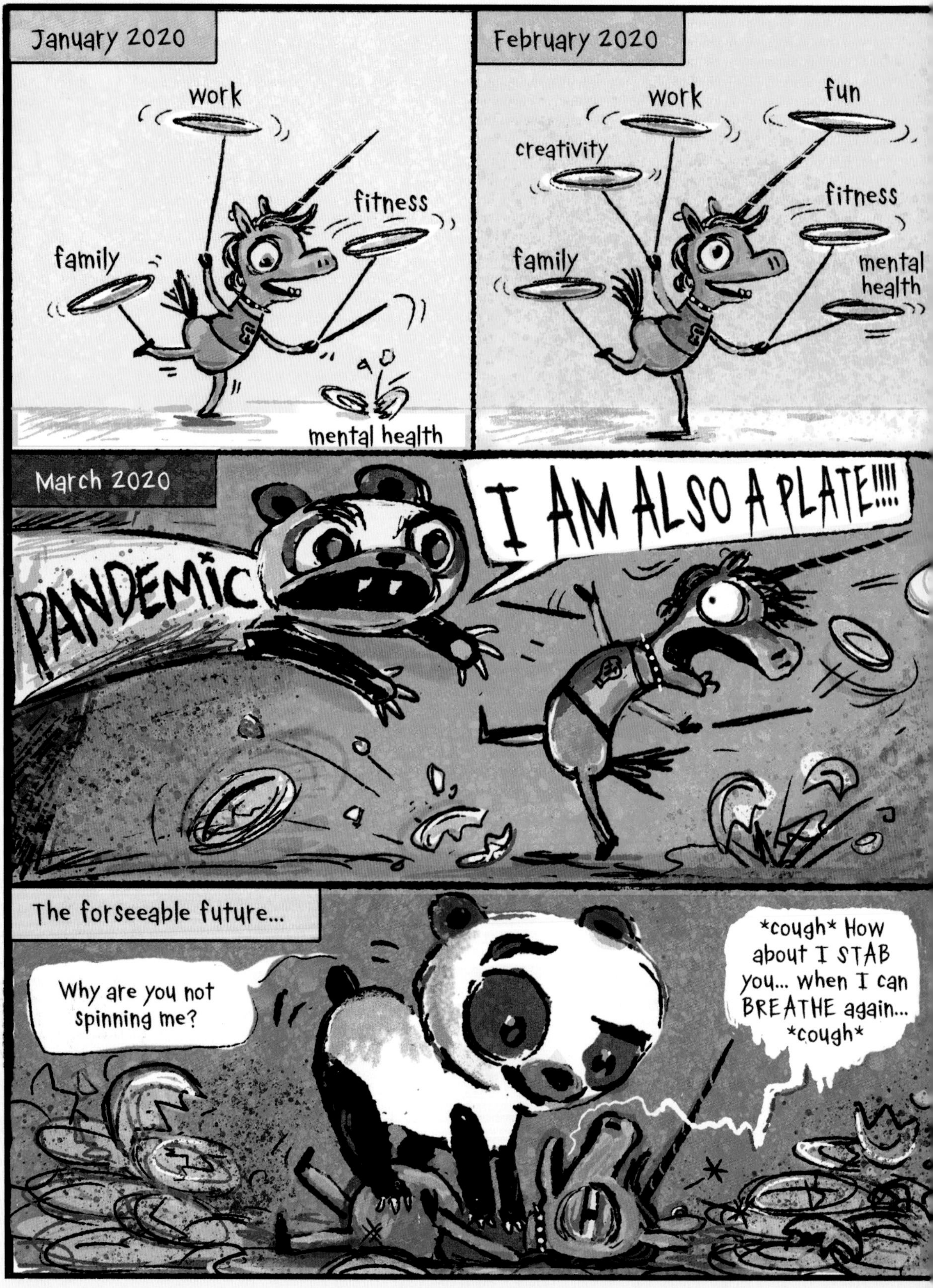
January 2020
work
fitness
family
mental health
February 2020
work
fun
creativity
fitness
family
mental health
March 2020
I AM ALSO A PLATE!!!!
PANDEMIC
The forseeable future...
Why are you not spinning me?
cough How about I STAB you... when I can BREATHE again... *cough*

Over My Head

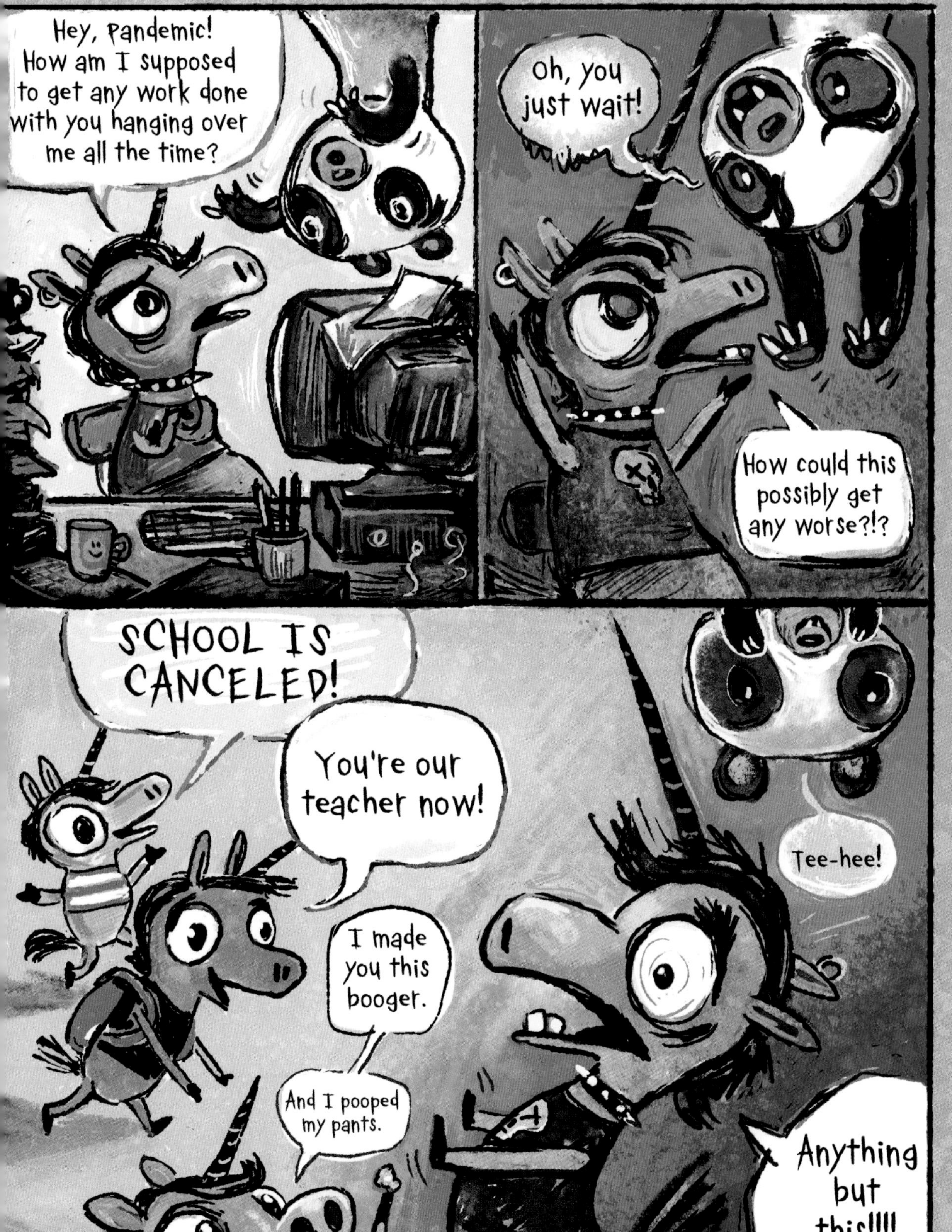

Hey, pandemic! How am I supposed to get any work done with you hanging over me all the time?
Oh, you just wait!
How could this possibly get any worse?!?
SCHOOL IS CANCELED!
You're our teacher now!
I made you this booger.
And I pooped my pants.
Tee-hee!
Anything but this!!!!

DEATH

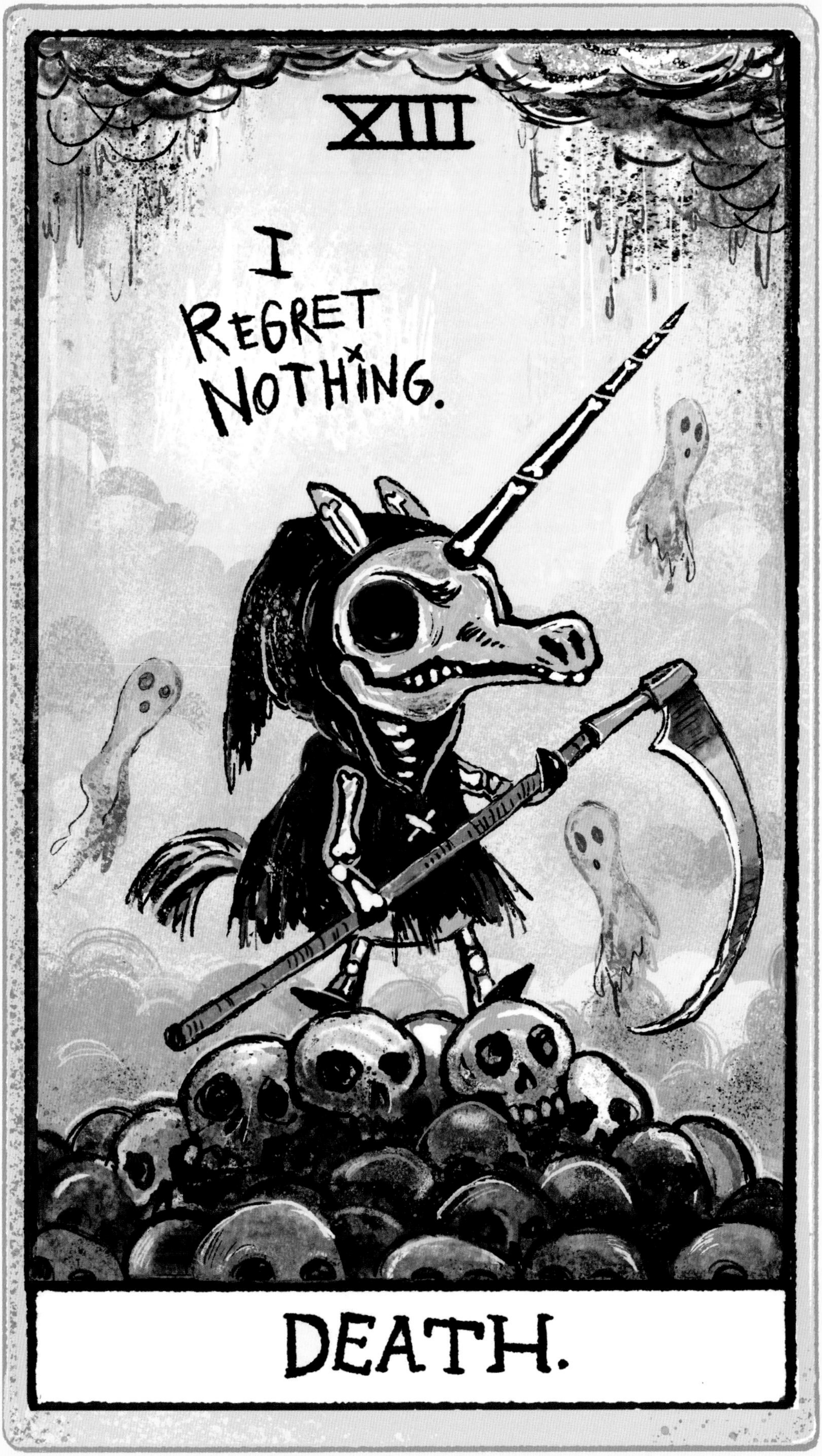
XIII
I REGRET NOTHING.
DEATH.

DEATH

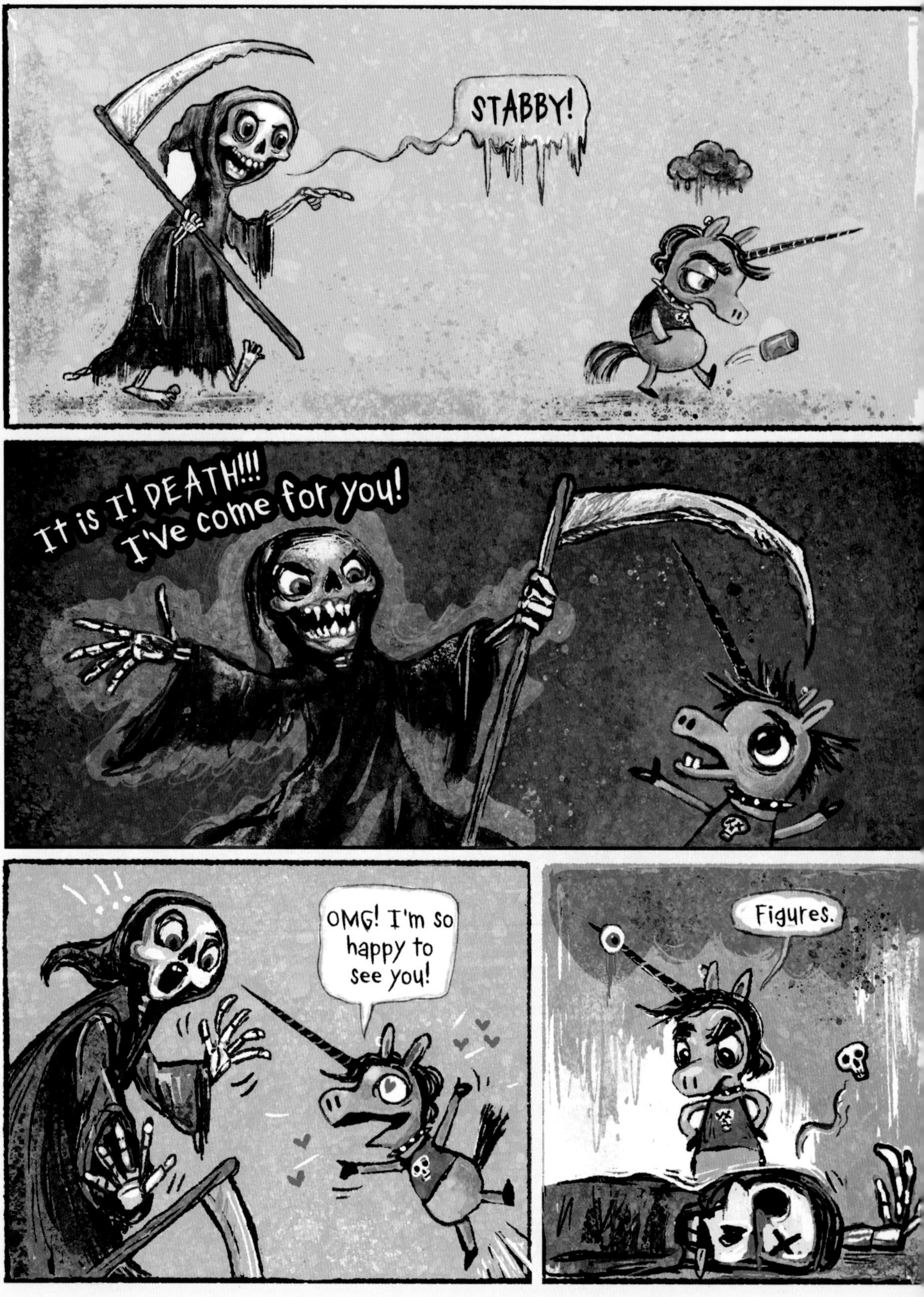
STABBY!
It is I! DEATH!!!
I've come for you!
OMG! I'm so happy to see you!
Figures.

Whatever doesn't kill you...

disappoints me.

END TIMES

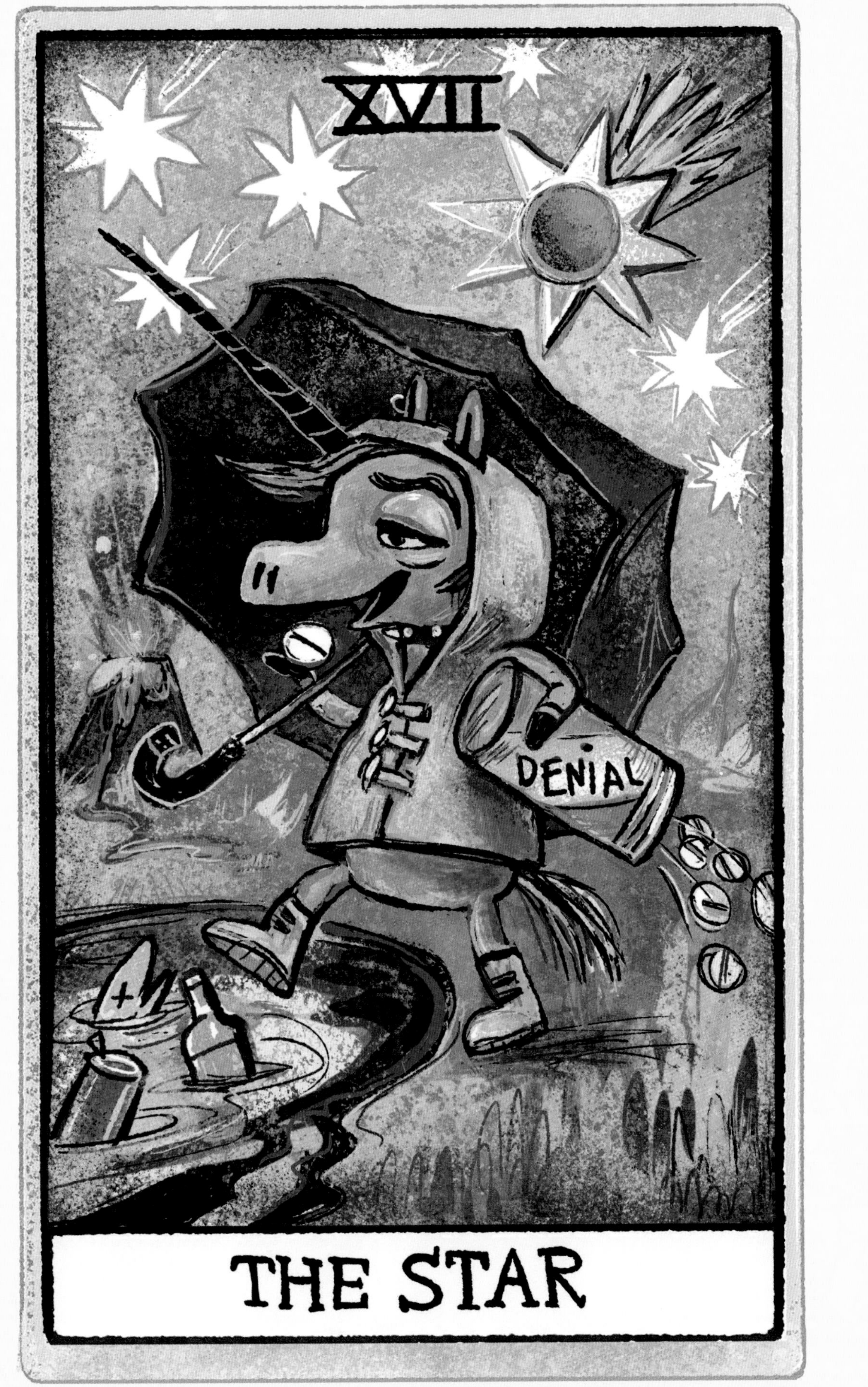
XVII
DENIAL
THE STAR

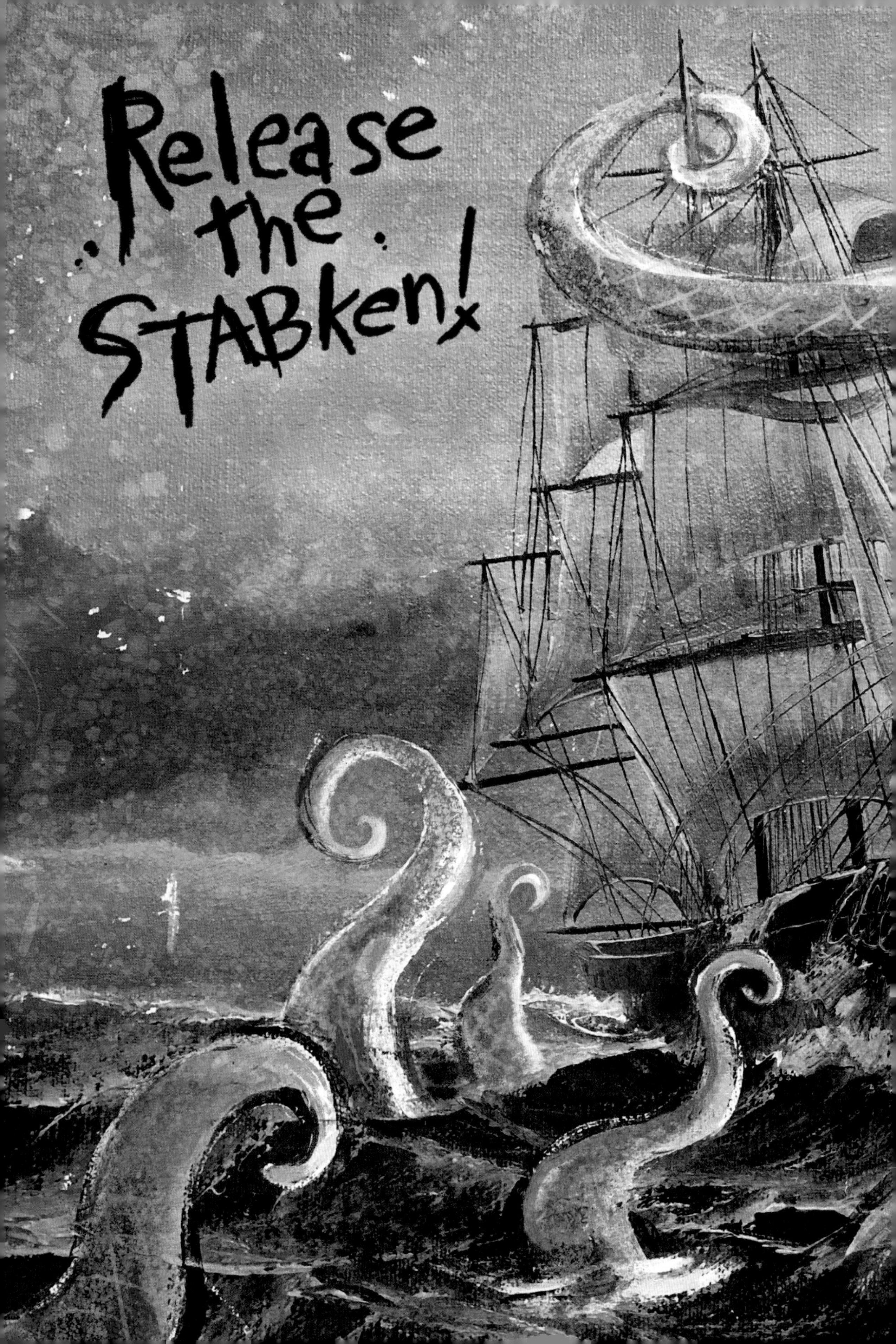
Release the STABken!

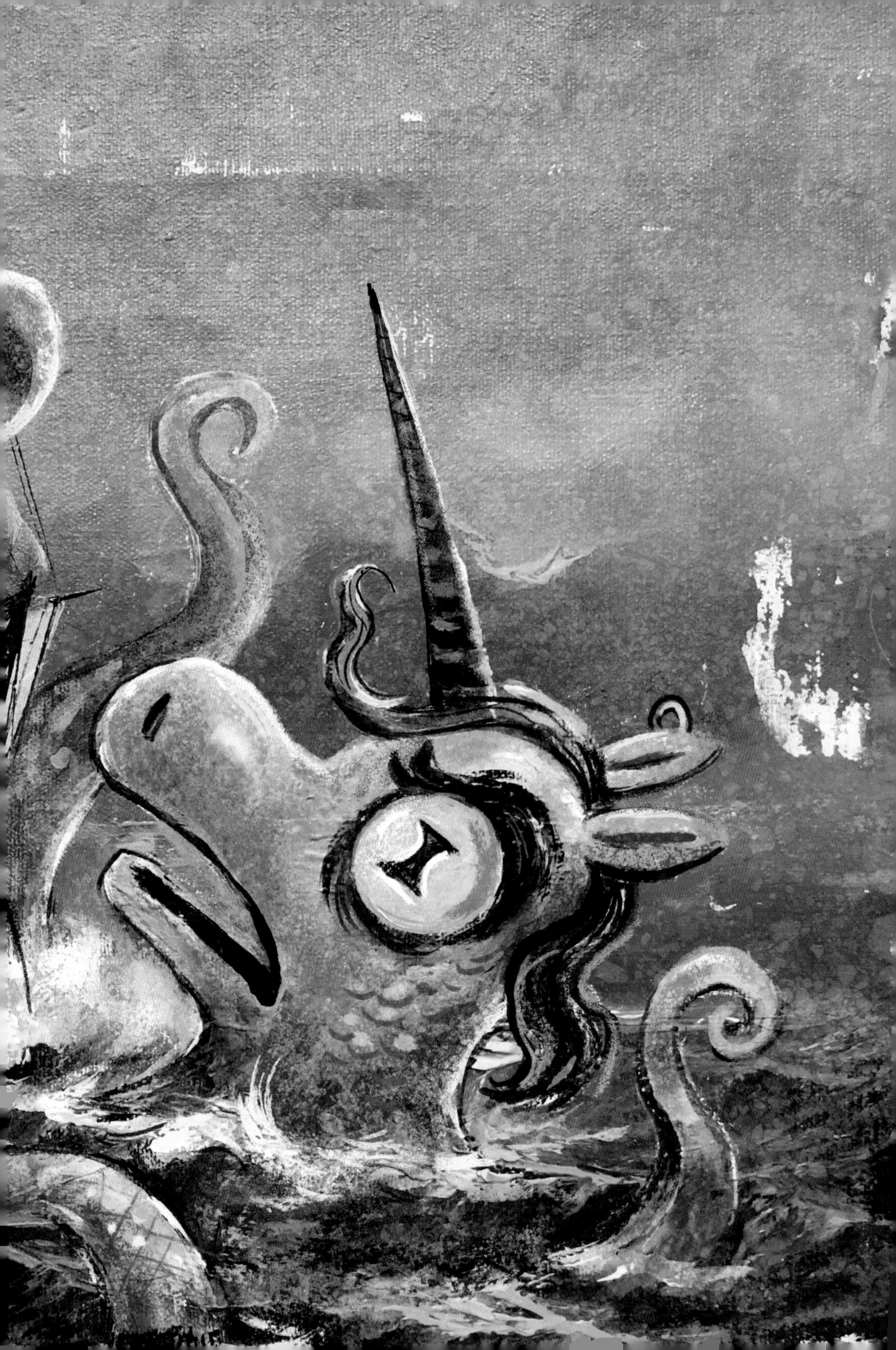

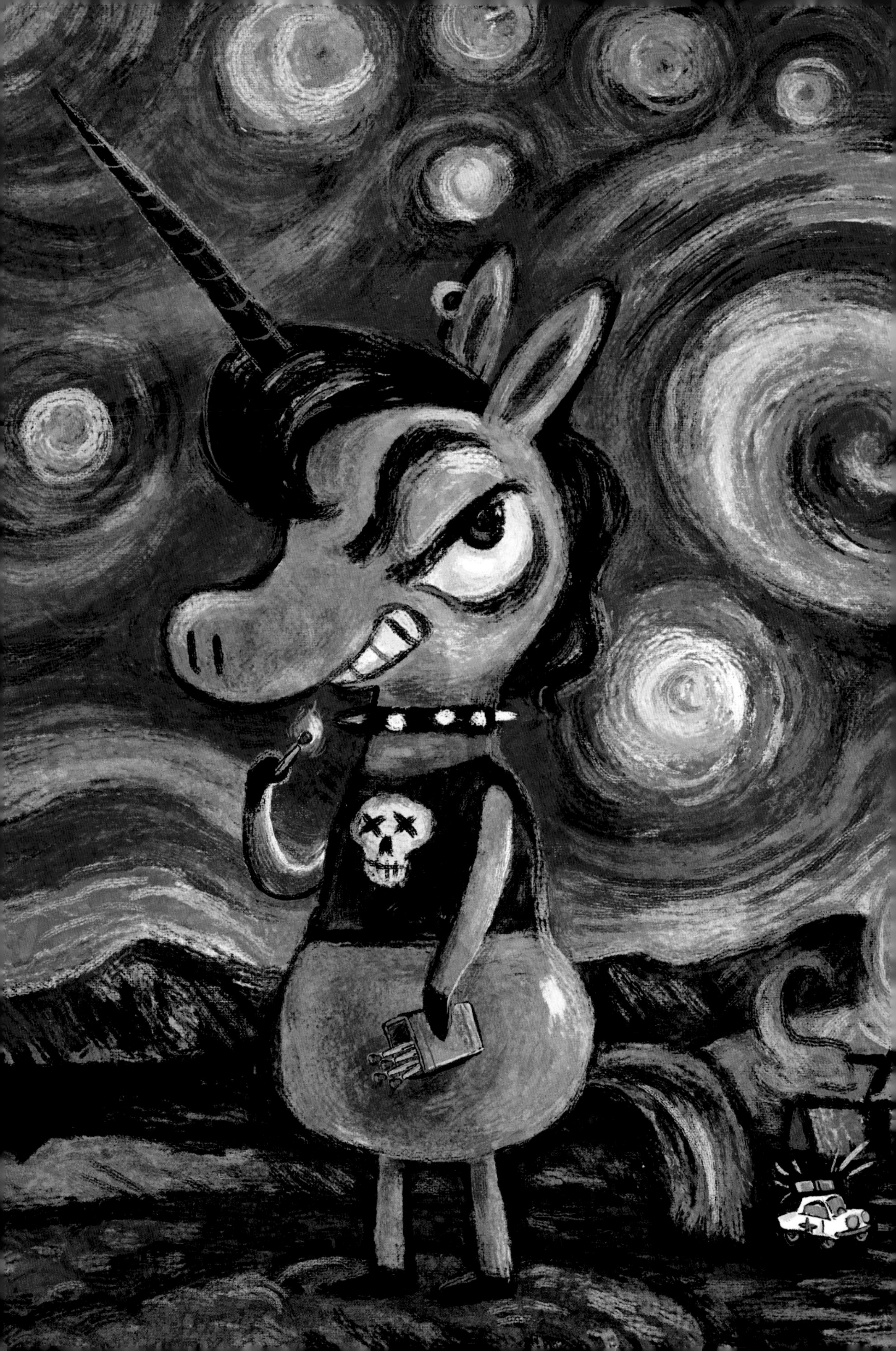

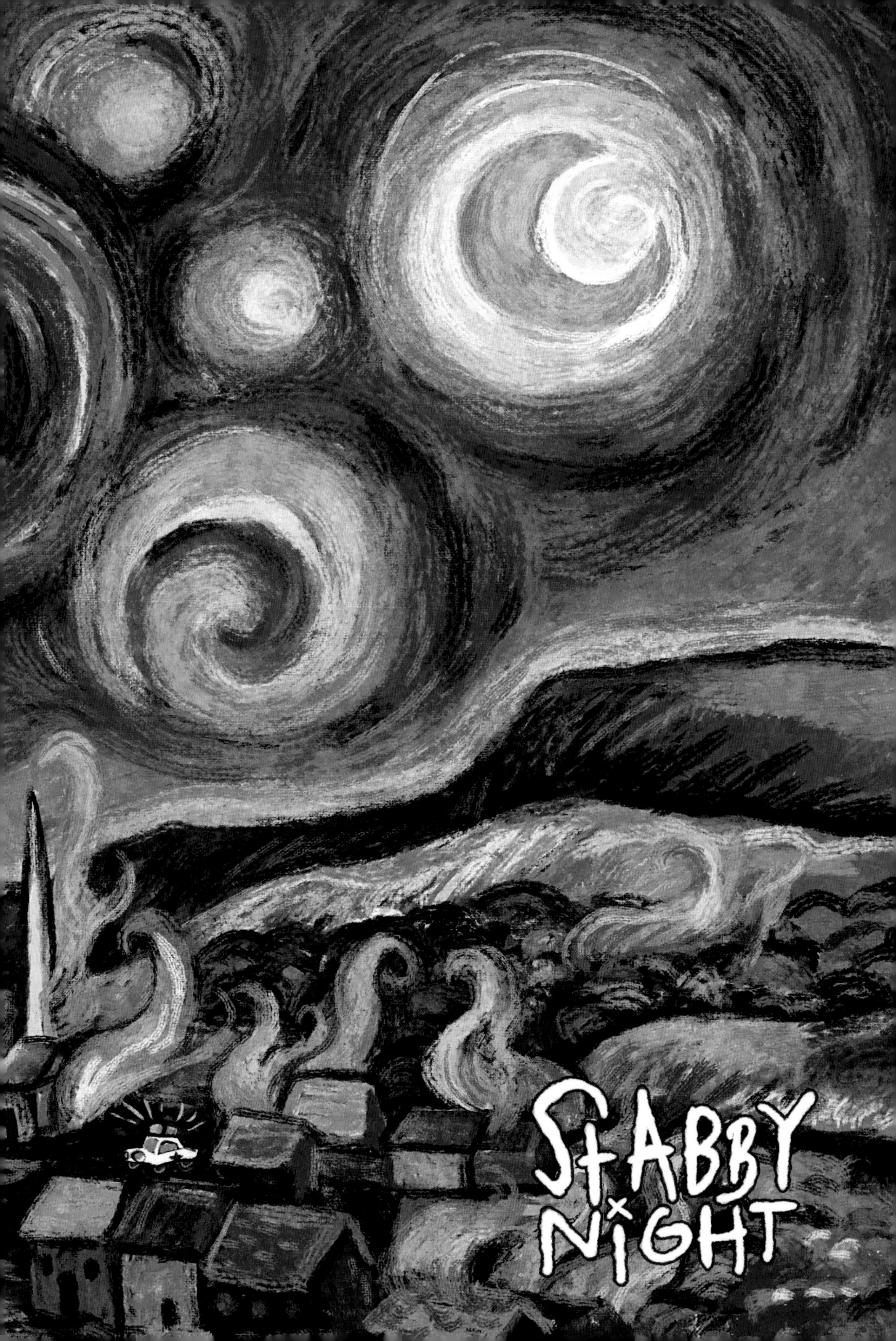
STABBY
NIGHT

How to draw STABBY:

1 Draw a circle for the head.

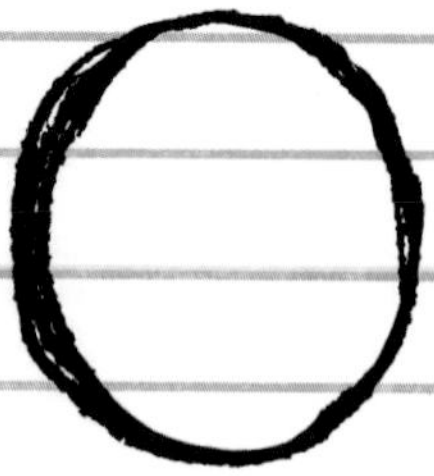

2 Make a triangle for the body.

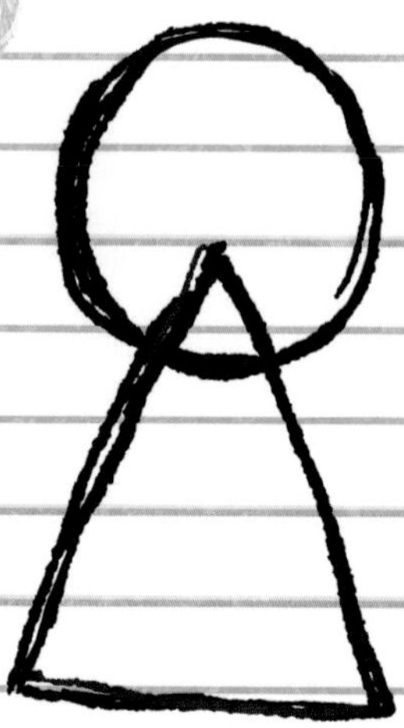

3 Use rectangles for ears, nose, arms, and legs.

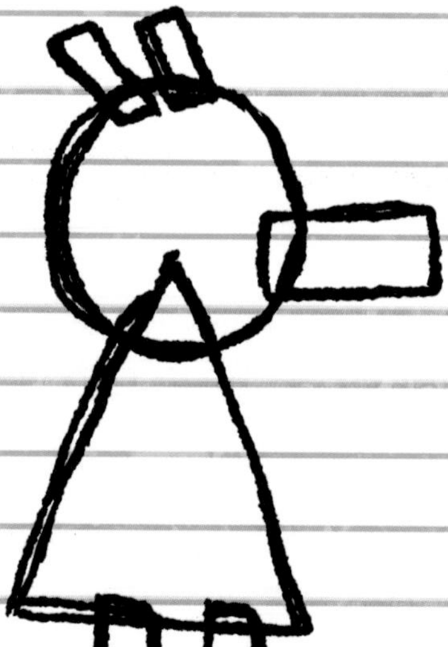

4 Draw hair, horn, and face. Erase extra lines.

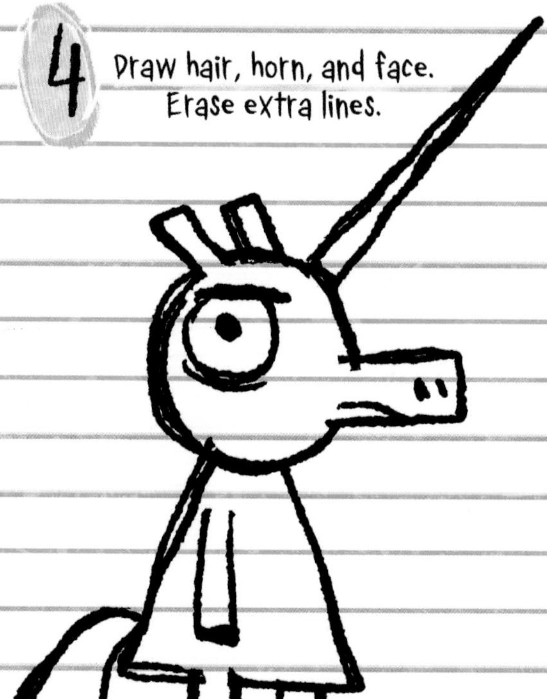

5 Add details.

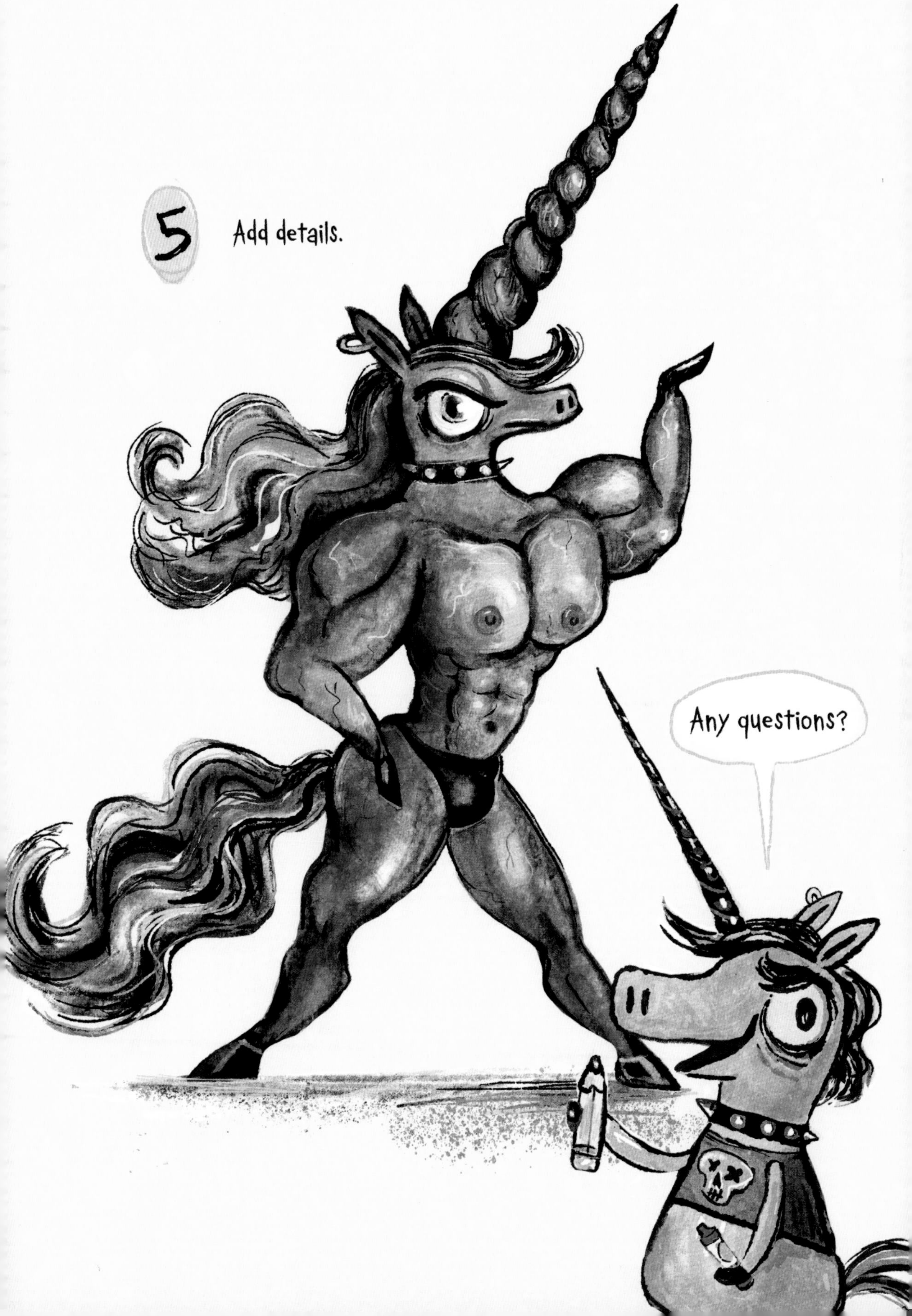
Any questions?

Published by Hermes Press, an imprint of Herman and Geer Communications, Inc.
Daniel Herman, Publisher
Eileen Sabrina Herman, Managing Editor
Troy Musguire, Production Manager
Alissa Fisher, Senior Graphic Design
Kandice Hartner, Graphic Design, Archivist
Erica McNatt, Copy Editor
2100 Wilmington Road
Neshannock, Pennsylvania 16105
(724) 652-0511
www.HermesPress.com; info@hermespress.com

This book is dedicated to all the weird little unicorns of the world. This stabs for you!

I want to thank:

- My supportive family, Steve, Finley, and Max. I love you! There's no one in the world I'd rather be quarantined without toilet paper with.

- My brilliant and hilarious critique group, the Squibby Bookcrafters — Anden, Amber, David, Dustin, Heather, and Stan. Your ideas, encouragement, honesty, and friendships make everything I do magically, maniacally better.

- My agent and friend, Timothy Travaglini at Transatlantic Agency. Your tenacity and dedication are unparalleled. There isn't enough ramen or soju in NYC to thank you enough!

- The Hermes Press team, especially Dan, Troy, and Sabrina, for championing the world's surliest unicorn right from the first stab.

First printing, 2021
LCCN Applied for: 10 9 8 7 6 5 4 3 2 1 0
ISBN 978-1-61345-205-9
From Dan, Louise, Sabrina, Jacob, Ruk, Noodle, and Ginger for D'Zur and Mellow
Printed in China

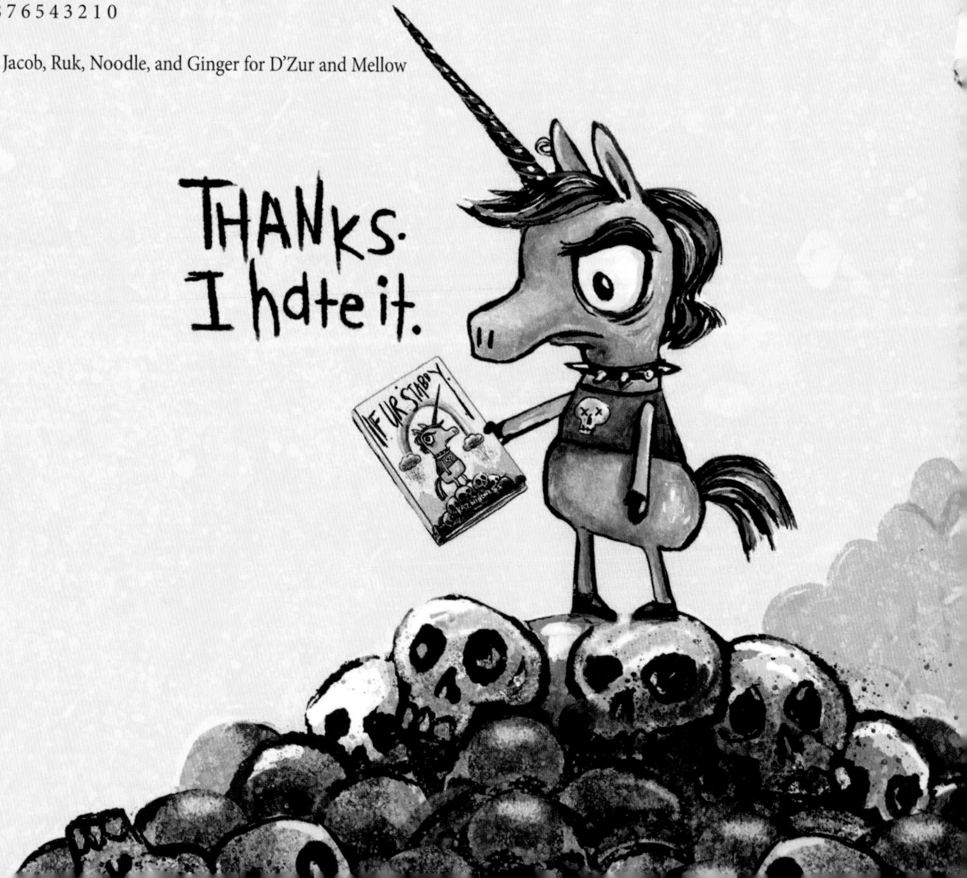
THANKS.
I hate it.
IF UR STABBY

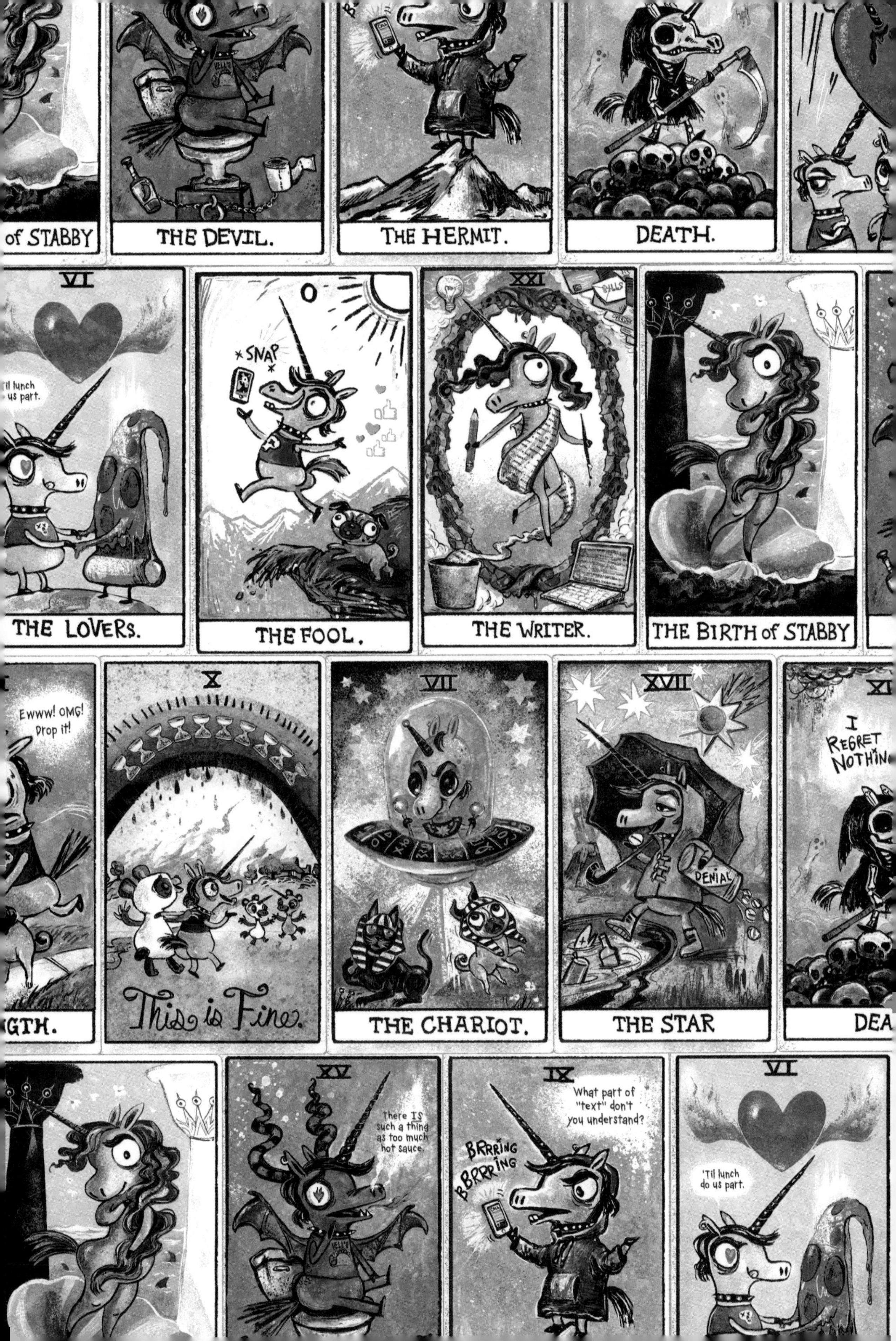
THE DEVIL.
THE HERMIT.
DEATH.
VI
THE LOVERS.
O
SNAP
THE FOOL.
XXI
BILLS
THE WRITER.
THE BIRTH of STABBY
Ewww! OMG! Drop it!
X
This is Fine.
VII
THE CHARIOT.
XVII
DENIAL
THE STAR
XV
There IS such a thing as too much hot sauce.
IX
What part of "text" don't you understand?
BRRRING
BRRRING
VI
'Til lunch do us part.

RTH of STABBY

THE DEVIL.

THE HERMIT.

DEATH.

THE LOVERs.

THE FOOL.

THE WRITER.

THE BIRTH of STABBY

RENGTH.

This is Fine.

THE CHARIOT.

THE STAR